Straight Talk About Today's Families

Straight Talk About Today's Families

Frances Presma
and
Paula Edelson

■® Facts On File, Inc.

Straight Talk About Today's Families

Facts On File, Inc.
11 Penn Plaza
New York NY 10001

Library of Congress Cataloging-in-Publication Data

Presma, Frances.
  Straight talk about today's families / Frances Presma and Paula Edelson.
    p. cm.
  Includes bibliographical references and index.
  Summary: Discusses the nature, importance, and challenges of being part of a family and explains ways to deal with family stress and dysfunction.
  ISBN 0-8160-3905-4
  1. Family—United States—Juvenile literature. 2. Teenagers—United States—Family relationships—Juvenile literature. 3. Problem families—United States—Juvenile literature. 4. Stress (Psychology)—United States. [1. Family. 2. Family problems.]
  I. Edelson, Paula. II. Title.
  HQ536.P725 1999
  306.85'0973—dc21   98-44901

Facts On File books are available at special discounts when purchased in bulk quantities for businesses, associations, institutions or sales promotions. Please call our Special Sales Department in New York at (212) 967-8800 or (800) 322-8755.

You can find Facts On File on the World Wide Web at
http://www.factsonfile.com

Text design by Cathy Rincon
Cover design by Smart Graphics
Printed in the United States of America

MP FOF 10 9 8 7 6 5 4 3 2 1

This book is printed on acid-free paper.

To our own families,
with love.

———

—FP, PE

Contents

1

Growing Up in Today's Families

It's pretty obvious that Ira* is adopted. He's black, and the rest of his family is white. His younger sister is adopted too, but at least she blends in. Ira has a lot of childhood memories of people asking his parents, "Who does this one belong to?" They would always respond the same way: "He's ours—cute, huh?" Ira really loves the way his parents don't make a big deal about skin color. Even so, there are times when he can't help feeling a little different from everyone else in his family.

Now that he's a teenager, Ira is thinking more and more about where he came from. Who was his real mother, and why did she give him up? Does he have brothers and sisters? Ira would love to know the answers to these questions, but he's not sure how to find them, or even if he should.

---

* Everyone identified by first name only in this book is a composite—a portrait drawn from details that come from many different people.

Eli is 16. He's never met his father. When he was little, he used to ask a lot of questions about his dad. He knows that his father was a musician and that he never really had a job. He also knows that his father left town before Eli was born. It's not easy for Eli's mom. She has to make enough money to support both of them. Once, when his mother was upset about money, she said that getting pregnant at age 20 was "a huge mistake." She didn't mean to hurt his feelings, but Eli was upset anyway.

Eli and his mom live about a block away from his grandfather Bud. Most days after school, Eli and Bud spend time together, rebuilding engines in the garage or playing chess on the porch. Being with his grandfather makes Eli really happy.

Annie's parents divorced five years ago. She was 10, and her sister, Lisa, was 8. Her mom and dad didn't fight much before that. They just seemed sad a lot of the time. When they split, they told the girls that they loved them but couldn't live together any more. Annie's dad bought a condo nearby, and she and Lisa see him pretty often—Wednesday dinners, weekends, and a lot during holidays. At first Annie missed having her dad around all the time, but both of her parents seemed happier after the divorce. Now her dad has a girlfriend who he says he really likes.

Annie's mom has a girlfriend too. Lin moved in last year. Before that, Annie's mom explained that she and Lin were in love and that they wanted to spend their lives together. That took some getting used to. But Annie likes Lin. She's funny and smart. And she seems to make Annie's mom happy. It is just weird sometimes to think of her mom being a lesbian. Kids at school throw that word around as an insult.

Marcy's parents are still together, but they fight every day. They argue about everything—money, "the kids," you name it. Sometimes they yell so loudly that Marcy's sure the neighbors can hear. And there have been some really bad scenes at home. One time her mother took an expensive vase and smashed it to the ground in anger. The whole situation has been really tough for Marcy to deal with. She thinks her older brother, Ben, is having a hard time with it too, but he won't talk about it with her. Luckily for Marcy, she can talk to her friend Annie, who's been really understanding.

Shira thinks her mother's boyfriend is kind of a jerk. When Rick and her mom started dating, he seemed OK, but since he moved in with them about two years ago, he hasn't been all that nice, either to Shira or to her mother. He's insulted both of them, and sometimes it seems like all he wants to do at the end of the day is drink a few beers and watch television.

Last month, when Shira had some friends over, Rick blew up at her. In a loud voice, he told her that she wore too much makeup and looked like a slut. He was drunk, of course. Shira wanted to die of embarrassment. Now, she doesn't bring any friends home. She always makes plans to meet them somewhere else—a friend's house or the mall.

Shira's not sure if she should tell her mother what she thinks of Rick. Sometimes she wonders why her mother puts up with him, but then she figures that if she didn't like him, she wouldn't be with him. Even so, Shira's worried. Lately Rick has been particularly nasty to her mother. It upsets Shira to hear him yelling. She hopes it's just a phase. Otherwise, Shira's not sure if she can live with them much longer.

The Nontraditional Family

Thirty years ago, the word *family* usually meant one thing: a married couple living with their biological or adopted children. That family structure is commonly called a "traditional," or "nuclear," family. In 1970, according to the U.S.

census, about 85 percent of all children under 18 lived in this kind of family. In addition, all members of this traditional family were almost always of the same race and religion. The man was usually the one with the job, and the woman generally stayed at home to raise the children.

Today, all that has changed. Most families in the United States are not traditional at all but fall under another category altogether—"nontraditional." A nontraditional family is a family that differs in some way from that of the traditional nuclear one. Many teenagers now live in families headed by only one parent. They may divide their time between their parents' homes following a divorce. They may live in "blended," or step-families after divorced or widowed parents remarry. Their parents may be openly homosexual, and children may be raised by a parent and his or her same-sex partner. Many families today are multiethnic or multiracial or involve a mixture of religions. An increasing number of teenagers are living with their grandparents or with caregivers other than their parents. And more likely than not, even those young people who are growing up in homes with two parents don't have a traditional "stay-at-home" mother. According to U.S. census figures, in 1991, nearly two-thirds of all married women with children worked outside the home. Fifty-nine percent of all children in the United States had mothers in the paid workforce.

Like traditional families, all nontraditional families share one important quality: They represent the single most important influence in their children's lives. Beyond that, though, they come in all shapes and sizes. Here are just a few of the ways nontraditional families are formed.

The Single-Parent Family

A single-parent family consists of children living with one parent. In 1994, 27 percent of all U.S. children lived in single-parent families, according to the Census Bureau, up from 12 percent in 1970. In actual numbers, single parents headed 11.5 million families in the United States in 1994. About 36 percent of these single parents had never been married, and 37 percent were divorced. The rest were separated from their partners or widowed.

There is a number of reasons for the sharp rise in the number of single-parent families. One is that the rate of divorce in the United States has increased tremendously since the 1960s. In 1960, the divorce rate was 2.2 per every 1,000 marriages. In 1996, it was 4.3 per 1,000, according to statistics compiled by the National Center for Health Statistics. Today, it is estimated that 40 percent of first marriages and 60 percent of second marriages will end in divorce. Another reason for the sharp rise of single parents is the number of out-of-wedlock births. Many of these never-married parents are or were teen mothers, whose numbers also have increased considerably since the 1960s.

In addition, there is a significant number of working women who are financially independent and single and are choosing to have children without getting married. Some of these women are having children biologically, and others are adopting. At one time married couples were always considered more desirable parents and therefore considered ahead of single people who wanted to adopt children, but today fewer adoption agencies are making that kind of distinction. Single people in America have the right to adopt in all 50 states, and courts are ruling with increasing frequency that the child's best interests, not the marital status of the adoptive parent, is the deciding factor in allowing an adoption to take place.

Blended Families

Blended families form when divorced or widowed parents remarry or start living with new partners. When they bring their children with them into their new relationship, they are said to be "mixing," or "blending," their families. These families are often called stepfamilies. According to the

Stepfamily Foundation, about 50 percent of American children under the age of 13 live in this type of situation.

Stepfamilies can be complex. If both stepparents have children, the children become stepsiblings. A child born into this blended family will be a biological half sibling to the stepsiblings. If both biological parents of a teenager have divorced and are living with new partners, that teenager may end up belonging to *two* blended families, with assorted stepsiblings and half siblings, and a complex network of relatives on all sides.

Unmarried Partners

Studies show that an increasing number of men and women are choosing to live together without being married, which is called cohabitation. For that reason, there are now laws protecting members of these families. In the event that an unmarried couple breaks up, each partner is entitled to a share of the "family" property and bears the obligation to support the children.

Homosexual Parents

Similarly, an increasing number of teenagers are living in families headed by homosexual parents. That doesn't necessarily reflect an increase in the number of homosexuals, but an increase in the number of parents who are openly identifying themselves as homosexual. There are no firm numbers on how many people are lesbian, gay, or bisexual in the United States, largely because people often keep their sexual orientation hidden. It is generally estimated that 1 in 10 people are homosexual, putting the national estimate at about 24 million. This means that there could be more than 6 million children with homosexual or bisexual parents in the United States.

In all likelihood, the number of children being raised by openly homosexual and bisexual parents is going to increase. In recent years many laws discriminating against homosexuals have gradually been eliminated, which means that more people are likely to be willing to become open about their sexual orientation. Annie's mother had her children biologically and naturally with her husband, then fell in love with a woman after her divorce. Other lesbians and bisexual women may choose to adopt or to become pregnant through artificial insemination (which is the introduction of a donor's sperm artificially, rather than through sexual intercourse).

Homosexuals cannot legally marry in the United States, so one member of a homosexual couple may forever be perceived to outsiders as an "unmarried partner." Like other unmarried partners, the nonbiological or nonadoptive partner does not have any legal rights to custody of children in the family unless they are expressly granted by the legal parent or caregiver, yet many homosexual couples actually bring children into their lives together, through birth or adoption, intending each to have equal "parental rights." Some are able to make this a legal reality by a process known as second parent adoption. In that way, the partner of a gay man or lesbian parent can adopt the children without terminating the parental rights of the biological or adoptive parent, and the children end up with two mothers or two fathers recognized under law. According to information provided by the National Adoption Information Clearinghouse, 21 states and the District of Columbia currently have legal precedents allowing for second parent adoptions for homosexual couples. In four states—Massachusetts, New Jersey, New York, and Vermont—the highest courts have ruled in favor of second parent adoptions, making them binding law.

There are some other types of families headed by unmarried partners. In some cases, for example, friends may live together to raise their children and offer one another the support of a family. This was the subject of a popular 1980s television show, *Kate and Allie*. In it, two divorced, single mothers who were platonic friends shared a house and coparented their children. For all intents and purposes, they were a family, of a sort that could be called an "intentional" family.

Grandparents as Parents

In some countries and cultures, it is not unusual at all for several generations of one family to live together in one home and for grandparents to share in the joys and challenges of raising the children. In the United States that situation is not quite as common, but it is becoming more so. In 1996, census figures show, nearly 6 percent of American children—one-fifth of them teenagers—lived with their grandparents. This figure is up from 4 percent in 1980. Moreover, more than one-third of these young people were being raised solely by their grandparents.

Grandparents who take over the raising of children do so for one of several reasons. It could be that there is a particular stress in the parents' lives, such as addiction to alcohol or drugs, incarceration, or illness, that is prohibiting them from being there for their children. This circumstance might also arise if a teenager whose family is moving away wants to stay put until finishing school, or if there are economic problems severe enough for the parent or parents' to give up custody of the children for an extended period of time.

Racially and Culturally Mixed Families

The members of racially and culturally mixed families are from more than one racial, ethnic, or cultural background. Their numbers are increasing in the United States today, for several reasons. More couples from different backgrounds are marrying or choosing to have children together, for one thing. When parents are of different races, their children are of mixed race, or biracial, although they may personally identify with one particular aspect of their racial heritage.

There were 1.3 million interracial married couples (representing all races) in the United States in 1994, according to the U.S. census. It is significant to note that until struck down by the U.S. Supreme Court in 1967 in the case of

Loving v. Commonwealth of Virginia, 16 states had laws prohibiting mixed-race marriages. In addition, according to the National Center for Health Statistics (NCHS), 52,232 births of children with one black and one white parent were recorded in 1991. That's an increase from 8,758 in 1968, the first year the center started keeping track of such figures.

Transracial Adoption

Another reason that the number of racially and culturally mixed families have increased so dramatically is that transracial and transcultural adoption has become very common in this country. These terms usually refer to the adoption by white parents of a child of color or from another country, but they can apply to any racial or cultural mix. One reason these adoptions have become so prevalent here is that multicultural families have become a much more accepted part of American society than they once were.

This is particularly true of adoption of African-American children by white parents, which has long been a controversial issue in the United States. In the 1960s, these types of adoptions began taking place because there were many more black children than white children available for adoption. At the same time, white adults willing to adopt a black child would often receive preference over black adults because, for the most part, white adults were in better economic standing. According to the National Adoption Information Clearinghouse, a branch of the U.S. Department of Health and Human Services, African-American families also felt "uncomfortable and unwelcome" with agencies staffed by mostly white social workers who were unfamiliar with the customs and values of the black community. Fearing prejudice and rejection, they were often reluctant to come forward as possible adoptive parents.

In the late 1960s, the National Association of Black Social Workers (NABSW) publicly objected to the adoption of black children into white homes. White parents, they said, could not raise African-American children with a proper sense of their racial and cultural heritage. Many public and private adoption agencies stopped such placements as a result.

That could change in the near future. Today, more than half of the 50,000 children in temporary foster homes who are waiting to be adopted are African American. In 1994, President Bill Clinton signed into law the Multiethnic Placement Act (MEPA), which is intended to help these children find suitable adoptive homes. Although acknowledging that same-race placements may be best for a child, the act prohibits federally funded agencies from using differences in race and culture as the deciding factor against the adoption. In December 1996, President Clinton announced another program, known as Adoption 2002, that aims to move children more quickly from foster homes into permanent adoptive homes and reduce the number of children in foster care dramatically by 2002. In spite of active recruitment of African-American families for children awaiting adoption, it is likely that at least some of them will be adopted transracially. No reliable statistics have been compiled as yet to trace the results of MEPA and the Adoption 2002 program.

Defining Yourself in Today's Families

There's no question about it—the notion of what makes up a typical American family has changed dramatically since the days when the traditional family was considered the norm. One thing that has not changed about families, however, is the influence they can have on their members. The family is, in fact, the single most important influence in a child's life. It is through their families that children first learn to interact with others, to share, to love and trust others, and to gain a feeling of self-worth.

When you were very young that influence was probably more intense than it is now. As a child, your family was the center of your world. Most likely you relied on family members to meet all of your needs—food, shelter, love, companionship. As a teenager, your world is bigger. You have more independence. You probably spend a lot more time at school and being with friends than you used to. You have your own tastes and your own opinions. They probably differ from your parents' in many ways.

All of that is part of growing up. Now that you're a teenager, you are in the midst of developing an individual identity. You are discovering who you are as a person, apart from your family. But family ties still matter. As a teenager, you just need your family in a different way than you did before. Like most teenagers, you probably still need your family for emotional support, guidance, and some level of acceptance of your choices. And like most teenagers, it's likely that you're still strongly influenced by what is going on at home.

Issues and Challenges

Another facet of life that all families share is the fact that challenges and issues are always certain to arise. Families with teenagers, for example, face the challenges posed by adolescence itself. Suddenly children who always did what they were told have become more independent beings capable of questioning authority and even rebelling against it at times. This can throw even the healthiest family for a loop—just because a teenager is ready to challenge parental authority and values on occasion, doesn't mean his or her parents are ready to be challenged!

All families will face unique challenges as well, such as the special needs of a child with a disability or an adopted teenager's curiosity about his or her origins. Take, for example, Ira, who is black, being raised in a white adoptive family. Because he is growing up in a white family, the development of racial identity is proving to be a special challenge for Ira. At this point, he doesn't know exactly where he fits.

Single-parent families may pose their own challenges. Eli, an only child of a single mother, often wishes that he had a father. He thinks another adult in the house would make things a lot easier for his mom. He's glad his grandfather lives so close to them because Bud is in many ways a father figure for Eli, but even so it's not the same as having a father at home.

Another challenge a family may have to face is a move. Today's families are very mobile and may move from place to place for professional or personal reasons. A move can remove support systems for all family members; it means leaving friends and often extended family (such as grandparents) behind. Teenagers in these families always need to find new systems of support—friends and trusted adults alike—as well as to stay connected with family and friends who have been left behind.

Divorce is one of the most common stresses facing teenagers today. A divorce is hard on everyone. If the adults involved can remain cooperative as parents, as Annie's parents have done, the breakup will be easier on their children. If they keep fighting, teenagers can go through an emotionally difficult time. Teens caught between warring parents, like Marcy, have to find ways of taking themselves out of the middle.

Following a divorce and remarriage, for instance, a teenager may find him- or herself with a complex network of relatives. There are one or two stepparents, who are new authority figures in a teen's life. In addition to full siblings, there may be some new stepsiblings and, after a time, half siblings. There may be a whole new set of extended family members. Again, the blended family can be a complex unit. Adjustment takes time, patience, and tact on everyone's part.

For teenagers like Annie, whose mother is a lesbian, the challenge may first be one of acceptance and understanding of her mom's sexual orientation. Then there are challenges that come from outside the family—what other people think, whether she will face ridicule at school. These issues arise for teens growing up in any nontraditional family.

It's true that all families face certain challenges and issues. The key is knowing how to cope with them and survive them in a healthy and constructive way. It is this ability that defines a healthy family. Teenagers who grow up in a healthy family atmosphere stand a good chance of being well prepared for adulthood, with the independence and confidence to thrive in the outside world. Unfortunately, there are some families who face serious, ongoing problems that prevent them from raising their children in a consistently healthy and loving way. These may range from alcohol and drug use by parents and caregivers to abuse and violence within the family. If this is the kind of family you're living in today, know that as a teenager you can't solve all your family's problems, but there are things you can do to help yourself get past them and thrive in spite of the situation at home. You'll learn more about this particular challenge in Chapters 4 and 5.

It's important to remember that any family can be a healthy one. This is true of two-parent and single-parent families, families that are interracial or intercultural, ones headed by homosexuals, and families that have been blended through divorce and remarriage. What all healthy families share is the ability to treat one another with respect, communicate well, support one another emotionally, share responsibilities, and handle stress and change well. You'll learn more about the ways family members relate to and communicate with one another in the next chapter.

2

The Healthy Family

Eli definitely pulls his weight at home. He's been doing his own laundry since he was eight, regularly does the household dusting and vacuuming, and cooks supper two nights each week. He actually likes cooking and is pretty good at it. Eli's mother teases him, saying "You'll make someone a wonderful wife some day." She also tells him that she appreciates the help.

To Eli, it seems like the least that he can do for his mother. He knows it's been hard on her, raising him alone. She's a nurse and often works double shifts in order to bring in extra money. Eli knows she's saving like crazy for his college education. Because she works such long hours, Eli's mom is away a lot, but Eli's grandfather Bud is always available to help out. He drives Eli to soccer practice and shows up at games when his mother can't. He even coached Eli's Little League team one year.

When they were little, Annie and her sister Lisa fought over everything—toys, TV shows, you name it. Every time they'd fight, their parents would say the same thing: "Work it out, or we'll work it out for you." Sometimes Annie and Lisa did work it out, and sometimes they didn't.

Annie is two years older than Lisa. She used to hate it when Lisa would tag along after her and her friends. Now they hang out together all the time. Annie actually considers Lisa one of her best friends. It's kind of funny because they're so different. Annie's a jock, and Lisa's anything but that. Annie's a neat freak, and Lisa's a total slob. Annie sometimes thinks that if they weren't sisters, they'd never be friends.

It seems to Marcy that her older brother, Ben, has changed a lot recently. They were pretty close when they were younger. Marcy was a tomboy back then and just wanted to do everything that Ben did. And he'd let her tag right along. When their family went camping, they'd share a tent and would stay up half the night reading comics by flashlight, talking, and making up stupid songs.

But now things are different. Ben's been running with a pretty wild crowd. They do a lot of partying, and Marcy knows Ben uses drugs. He hardly talks to her—or anyone else in the family—anymore. Marcy feels both sad and angry about that. She's sad because she misses the times she and Ben had together. And she's angry because she feels like Ben is shutting her out during a difficult time—their parents' relationship is getting worse by the day, and things are ugly. Marcy really needs Ben to be there for her.

For as long as he can remember, Ira's family has belonged to a special club. They meet once a month for potluck suppers or picnics. All the member families in the club are, like Ira's, racially mixed. Many of the kids were adopted transracially.

Once, a few years back, Ira asked his father why they all went to the club. His dad said that when they adopted Ira, they knew their family would look different and be different from a lot of others they knew. The other members of the club helped them to feel like part of a community. Sometimes Ira thinks the club is a little silly. All he has in common with some of these kids is the fact that they're black, or a different color from their parents.

Families that are healthy come in all shapes, sizes, and structures. Every family is different, with its own history, culture, and way of functioning. But as you know by now, healthy families do share certain qualities.

In general, healthy families do far more than just meet their members' basic needs for food, shelter, and clothing. In any number of ways, people who are in healthy families offer one another the following, less tangible benefits.

1. **Respect.** Family members honor one another's feelings, possessions, and privacy. They don't listen in on one another's phone conversations, for instance, or borrow personal items without asking. They don't bully or put one another down.
2. **Emotional Support.** Family members can share their good and bad times, their victories and failures. Emotional support can be provided in any number of ways—simply by listening, or by offering sincere praise, thanks, or assistance. When a family member needs space, or time alone, the others provide it.
3. **Structure.** Healthy families also support their members by giving their lives structure. From a parent's perspective, this may involve making household rules and setting limits for their children, such as saying no to staying out very late or not allowing them to go to a party on a school night. Siblings can set similar limits for one another. Ira's younger sister, for example, was really struggling with an essay assignment for her

seventh-grade English class. In a moment of despera-
tion, she asked Ira if she could copy the essay he had
written when he was in seventh grade. Ira said he didn't
think that was such a great idea. Instead, he helped her
flesh out her own ideas for a paper and gave her
research tips. He helped her learn to do her own work.

4. **Cooperation.** Sharing chores and other household
responsibilities allows everyone in the family to
make some sort of contribution. It promotes a feeling of value and connection. Many families link
responsibilities to privileges. If Annie and Lisa want
to have friends over on a Saturday night, for example, they might be expected to clean the family room
before and after the party.

5. **Communication.** A commitment to communicating
clearly and effectively is one of the most important
values a healthy family should have. Communicating
well with one another does not mean that family
members agree all the time. Conflict is inevitable
whenever people live together. What members of
healthy families are able to do, though, is to listen to
one another and look for creative, constructive ways
to resolve these conflicts.

6. **Managing change.** Today's families go through all
sorts of changes that require significant adjustments—moves, job promotions and losses, divorce,
remarriages, births, and deaths, to name a few.
Change can often be stressful as family members
struggle with new roles, responsibilities, and pressures from in- and outside the family. The members
of a healthy family weather these pressures until the
stress passes by listening to one another, offering
emotional support, and filling in for one another in
appropriate situations. That's what Annie and Lisa did
for each other during their parents' divorce, and it
drew them closer together.

Another very important quality most healthy families share is the ability to give its members the freedom to grow. This is especially important for teenagers, who almost always need the support and love of their families in order to have the self-esteem and strength to become independent and fair-minded individuals in their own right. The initial and most important source of that support usually, but not always, comes from the teenager's parent(s) or caregiver(s). It can also come from a sibling, from a member of the extended family, or sometimes from a trusted adult who is not a relation but serves as a role model. This is especially true of young people who are growing up in dysfunctional families.

How Healthy Families Communicate

Perhaps the most important quality healthy families share is the ability to communicate with one another actively and constantly, through both good and bad times. Effective communication will help any relationship, but it is particularly important among family members. Coordinating the details of everyday family life—who needs to use the car when, what to have for dinner, whose turn is it to clean the bathroom—all involve communication. Bigger issues, from discussing career goals to family problems, require communication. And as you mature and develop opinions of your own, you will want them to be heard and respected by your family members. Communicating them clearly is the best way to ensure that you have a voice. Effective communication also helps to reduce misunderstandings that can lead to serious arguments.

Here are some basic techniques for effective communication.

1. **Try not to be overly negative.** When talking with other family members, avoid criticism and ridicule. Nobody likes to be personally attacked, put down, or treated with sarcasm. It doesn't matter if the person is 15 or 50.

2. **Use "I" messages, and not "you" messages** that can easily be taken as personal attacks. In his book You and Your Adolescent, psychologist Lawrence Steinberg offers this formula for "I" messages: "When you_____[describe the event nonjudgmentally], I feel_____[describe your feelings] because_____[describe how that behavior affected you]." "I" messages take practice and thought. After a while, though, they become second nature. If your sister leaves the bathroom a mess, for example, it may be tempting to say, "You always leave the place a mess. You're just an unbelievable slob." You are justified in being angry about having to clean up after her, but your message is likely to put her on the defensive. She might refuse to listen further or attack you for the way you left the bedroom. If you use an "I" message, such as "When you left the bathtub dirty and the drain clogged with hair, I felt angry, because I had to clean it up and ended up missing the school bus," your sister is more likely to understand how her actions caused you unnecessary inconvenience.

3. **Listen "actively."** Here are some tips.
   - Pay attention. Face the speaker and make eye contact.
   - Observe body language, both your own and the other person's. Is the person speaking softly but indicating, with crossed arms and twitching eyes, that he or she is really angry? Are you leaning back in your chair with arms crossed as if you don't care about what is being said?
   - Don't interrupt.
   - Try not to get defensive if your behavior is the subject of the discussion.
   - Talk to the other person about what he or she has just said to make sure you understand and to help clarify the point.

Resolving Conflict

Effective communication will help reduce conflict and resolve it when it occurs, but it won't eliminate it entirely. Whenever people live closely together and interact on a daily basis, conflict is inevitable. In families, it often arises around everyday issues, such as chores, sharing space, and personal habits. Common areas of conflict between teenagers and their parents and caregivers also include clothing, dating, schoolwork, choice of friends, and sex.

Conflict isn't always a bad thing. Being forced to resolve an ongoing issue can pull people out of ruts by forcing them to find new solutions to problems. It can become damaging, however, if the conflict is not dealt with properly. When this happens, anger is likely to occur. Remember anger is a natural emotion, and it's one that can often be expressed constructively if those involved are able to resolve their differences through honest and effective discussion. Here are some suggestions on how this can be achieved.

1. Focus on the problem, as opposed to attacking the person. Avoid name-calling and other forms of attack.
   - Define the problem. For example, let's say you and your brother would both like to use your parents' car that night. You may define the issue as "We both want to use the car."
   - Explore how each of you views the problem, to see and understand the other's point of view. Your brother may see the problem as "You got to use it last night, so now it's my turn." You may see it as "If I don't get to the library this evening, I can't finish my report."
   - Keep an open mind. Try to understand the other's point of view.
   - Practice your communication skills, using "I" messages, listening, and summarizing.
2. Focus on needs and feelings, not outcomes. For example, instead of saying, "I want to use the car," which is the outcome you desire, you could say, "I need to get

to the library to finish my report." This leaves the door open to solutions other than just taking the car.

3. Try to find solutions that allow you both to win. Your brother might agree to drop you off at the library and pick you up.

Jeffrey and Carol Rubin, authors of *When Families Fight,* emphasize the importance of the human need to save face—to look "competent, strong, proud, effective" and not to look like a fool. When people are angry, they may dig in their heels in order not to feel or look foolish. If you can acknowledge that tendency in yourself and in others, it may help you avoid fights that get out of hand.

The Rubins stress that there are certain things one can do to help resolve the conflict without losing face. Flip a coin to solve the car problem if you can't resolve it any other way. That will take it out of the realm of being personal and leave the decision to chance. If the conflict continues and tempers begin to flair, it's sometimes a good idea to take a break from it. Take a walk by yourself or with a friend. This will give you time away from the argument and give you and your brother the opportunity to cool down.

Even if you feel that you are being treated like a child and that the person you are fighting with is being unfair or getting overly personal in the argument, taking a mature, fair approach to handling conflict can make a huge difference to the outcome. Learning how to communicate and resolve conflicts early on, and practicing on your family, will be invaluable in all your relationships in life.

Communicating effectively is one of the keys to living in a healthy family. And it's a quality that all members—in all kinds of families—should use consistently with one another. The rest of this chapter will give you an idea of the complex relationships that exist within families, as well as some unique situations that some of today's families may experience.

Adult Caregivers

The adult caregivers of a family may be biological, adoptive, or foster parents, stepparents, grandparents, or a parent's same-sex partner. In general, they are anyone who is directly raising a child and with whom the child has established close ties. These caregivers are the individuals who provide the most significant love, protection, and care for the family's children. If the relationship between a child and a caregiver (such as a parent) is a healthy one, that child will begin to develop a positive self-image and a sense of self-worth. If, on the other hand, a child is neglected or treated harshly, that child will have a harder time developing these characteristics. The adult caregivers are also the ones who provide a child with his or her first role models with whom to identify. Again, if the caregiver is loving and giving, that identification will be much more healthy than if the caregiver is neglectful or abusive.

As you know by now, developing a self-image and identity independent from your parents is a normal part of adolescence. This makes the caregivers' influence on you now a little different from what it was when you were younger. But that doesn't mean parents and caregivers cease to be important. Teenagers don't need their parents as much as children do for protection and to provide basic needs, but most still need their love, acceptance, approval, and guidance in developing values and setting goals. Studies on adolescent behavior show, for example, that teenagers who remain close to their parents or caregivers are better equipped to resist peer pressure to do drugs or get involved with crime than are those who do not.

Single Parents

As you learned in the first chapter, a significant number of today's families are headed by single parents. This type of family differs from many two-parent families in certain important ways.

One parent, for example, means one income. Although many of today's families face financial problems, they are particularly common in single-parent homes. Eli knows that his mother struggles to make ends meet. She doesn't complain, but he can see how hard she works to give him the things that some of his other friends take for granted. Eli tries to make it easier for her by not asking for too many extras and helping out with the chores. It is not uncommon for young people in single-parent families to take on a greater share of household responsibilities than some of their friends in two-parent families. As a result, some of them, like Eli, feel more responsible and self-sufficient than many of their friends.

Another way in which single-parent families differ from those that are headed by two parents is in the relationship that forms between the parents and children. While a child who is in a two-parent home frequently has a close bond with one parent or with both, the truth is that when a couple raises children together, a large part of that couple's emotional energies are directed toward one another. In a healthy relationship, they "coparent," making household rules and decisions together and working together to make sure these rules and decisions work. Because single parents don't have a regular, live-in partner with whom they have this particular dynamic, the relationship that forms between them and their children is often particularly close and emotional. For the most part this is very healthy, but it can sometimes challenge their ability to set limits. Shoshana Alexander is a single mother and author of In Praise of Single Parents. She writes of the challenges she faces raising her son alone: "All parents struggle with issues of loving and limiting, but within our single-parent family, there is no automatic hierarchy of two adults defining the power structure, there is no one to advise me as to whether I am being too strict or too lenient, there is no alternate support for either of us."

In the absence of another adult, Alexander writes, single parents may use their children as sounding boards, talking openly about personal problems—jobs, finances, even sex. While a certain level of openness is appropriate, too much can be hard on teenagers, who may "feel very vulnerable, aware of their contribution to the burden but with no ability to help solve the problem." Young people, she says, need to see parents solve their problems themselves, or with outside help, instead of taking on their parents' burdens. Ultimately, single parents in healthy families are able to maintain appropriate emotional boundaries. They confide in their children but do not overburden them—kids need to be kids. Instead, they turn to other adults, such as friends and relatives, for support and help.

Extended Family and Other Adults

Many children and teenagers form close bonds with adults other than their parents. For example, according to *Grandparents/Grandchildren: The Vital Connection*, a 1981 book by Arthur Kornhaber, a child psychiatrist, and Kenneth Woodward, "the attachment between grandparent and grandchild is second in emotional power and influence only to the relationship between parents and children." There is a difference, though: A lot of natural tensions that arise between parents and children do not occur between grandparents and grandchildren. Eli and Bud, for example, share a passion for old cars. They spend a lot of time together rebuilding them, and Eli loves to listen to Bud's stories about growing up during the years of World War II. Eli loves his mother dearly, but he finds he can relax with Bud more than he can with her.

Grandparents can be a source of unconditional love and acceptance that are essential to a child's self-esteem. They can help children gain an appreciation of their heritage. By sharing family stories, grandparents can even help teenagers understand why their own parents behave in certain ways.

Grandparents form part of the extended family, which also includes aunts, uncles, cousins, and other kin. In many cultures and societies it is common for extended family members to live together in one home. That is relatively uncommon in the United States today, although some cultural groups are more likely to continue the practice than others. But whether or not they live together, contact with a network of grandparents, aunts, uncles, and other relatives can be a positive source of support for a teenager.

Grandparents as Parents

An increasing number of grandparents are directly raising their grandchildren because the parents cannot. The parents may be ill, incarcerated, addicted to drugs, still in school if they are teenagers, or just going through tough times. In some cases, the grandparents may be temporary caregivers for their grandchildren. In others, the arrangement may be permanent.

Grandparents are often the best nonparent caregivers for their grandchildren because of their strong emotional connection. They can be an important source of support and stability. But everyone will need time and possibly help to adjust to the new arrangement. Children and teenagers may have to deal with feelings of loss, sadness, confusion, or anger surrounding the traumatic event that brought it about. The grandparents themselves may not have been expecting to suddenly become caregivers again. They may have their own feelings of anger or sadness about the situation. Financially they may not have been prepared to raise a "second" family.

Other issues can arise from the age gap between grandparents and grandchildren. It may be challenging to connect on such issues as dating, sexuality, clothes, and music. It may even be hard for grandparents to help with homework—school and technology have changed a lot over the years. But none of these is insurmountable. An increasing number of school and community support groups help grandparent-headed families make the necessary adjustments. An awareness of issues and possible areas of conflict and a commitment to resolving them aid in adapting to new situations.

Unmarried Partners

Partners of adult caregivers can play significant roles in the lives of children and teenagers within the family. The quality of the relationship between a partner and a child will depend greatly on the quality of the relationship between the two adults. If the relationship is stable, loving, and long term, the partner is likely to take a strong interest in a child and share his or her time, interests, and activities. Strong emotional bonds can form as a result. Ultimately, the status of the partner in the child's life will be determined over time. Although some may remain distant, forever just "partners," many others become friends, advisers, authority figures, and, for all intents and purposes, full caregivers much like stepparents. Issues relating to a child's adjustment to his or her caregiver's partner are similar to those involved in blended families. Those issues are explored in greater detail in Chapter Three.

Siblings

"It is with our brothers and sisters that we learn to love, share, negotiate, start and end fights, hurt others and save face." That's how Jane Mersky Leder sums up the importance of the sibling relationship in her book *Brothers and Sisters: How They Shape Our Lives*. From your earliest years, your biological or adopted siblings have likely been, at times, your favorite playmates and at others, the biggest pains in your neck. In these roles, they have helped you learn how to develop friendships and relationships with people outside your family.

If you have them, your siblings are your peers within your family. There are certain things that you are probably more comfortable discussing with a brother or sister than with your parents. When you have a fight with a friend, your sibling is probably going to hear about it. You may physically move away from friends or from a divorcing parent, but chances are that your siblings will make the move with you. And in periods of family stress, such as a divorce or a move, siblings may be a unique source of emotional support. Annie and Lisa, for example, started to pull together when their parents split and especially when they later found out their mother was a lesbian. They talked about a lot of things that they couldn't really share with anyone else at the time.

How Siblings Relate

Like parents and caregivers, siblings have a definite role in shaping a teenager's identity, or sense of self. A loving, positive relationship with a brother or sister is likely to be beneficial to a teenager's self-esteem. Excessive teasing or aggression from a sibling, on the other hand, can be damaging.

A lot of factors may influence the way siblings get along with one another. One of the most important of these factors are the parents or caregivers, who in a healthy family will encourage a sense of uniqueness in each of their children, while promoting a sense of cooperation and mutual caring among them.

Another factor that can influence the relationship between siblings is change. This is especially true of the changes—especially extreme ones—that sometimes take place during the teenage years. This is what happened to Ben and Marcy. Ben, who once shared his interests and his time with his younger sister, doesn't really want to be with her now. And on the flip side, Marcy is finding that the things she's pretty sure Ben is doing—like using drugs and staying out all night all the time—are not really activities she particularly likes or respects.

On the other hand, Annie and Lisa really found each other once they became teenagers and were able to appreciate each other's differences and to enjoy each other's company. Whether they grow closer or farther apart during this time, though, the teenage years almost always bring new dynamics to the sibling relationship. "Adolescence often requires that siblings stop and reevaluate their relationship," writes Jane Mersky Leder of this time of life. "Siblings either learn to accept one another as independent individuals with their own sets of values or behaviors, or cling to the shadow of the brother and sister they once knew."

Sibling Rivalry

Of course, every sibling relationship has its share of ups and downs. There are very few people with a brother or sister who have not been teased one day, then helped out the next. And there are other natural tendencies and dynamics that tend to form between siblings. You have probably heard, for example, the term *sibling rivalry*. In early childhood, that generally refers to the competition that goes on between siblings for their parents' attention and affection. Later on, it can include the ways siblings compare themselves and compete with one another. A certain amount of sibling rivalry may be healthy. It may push siblings to excel in academics or other areas. But if taken to extremes, which happens infrequently but does occur, this rivalry can be damaging. It can hurt not only one or both sibling's sense of confidence and self-esteem—if there's always a sense that one sibling is constantly falling short of the other—but their relationship as well.

Some psychologists suggest that one way siblings can reduce their rivalries is to focus on their differences rather than their similarities. They identify separate areas in which they excel and that define them. Annie, for example, may be the jock in the family, but Lisa is gifted musically—she can play just about any instrument she picks up. Annie can barely carry a tune, and Lisa can hardly catch a ball. Because Annie and Lisa both have talents that they are proud of, they are able to admire the other one's gifts without feeling overshadowed or insecure.

Stepsiblings

Stepsibling relationships are formed when parents remarry following a death or a divorce. If stepsiblings come into one another's lives early on, their relationships with each other are often no different from biological siblings or adopted siblings. If not, it may be a unique relationship for several reasons.

For one thing, because stepsiblings become related to one another so quickly, there is sometimes little time to get used to the idea of having another sister or brother around. This lack of preparation may especially affect young children who do not have biological siblings. A child who is about to become a biological sibling might have a difficult time getting used to sharing his or her parent's attention but often has time to adjust to this change—or at least talk about it—during his or her mother's pregnancy. A child who has not gone through this experience and quickly gains a stepsibling may find the change much harder to accept. In addition, because they come from different family backgrounds, stepsiblings may have grown up with very different customs, values, and styles. And if they are all from divorced families, they may not all live together all the time. When they are together, they may find themselves in a different sibling position—third, instead of first—with different family expectations and responsibilities.

Not all teenagers are happy about finding themselves in a stepfamily. They may still be angry or sad about the event that made this new situation possible—their parents' divorce or the death of a parent. They may resent the new changes in their lives. If, for example, a girl always had her own room and suddenly has to share one with a stepsister, it can be a big adjustment. On the other hand, having a stepsibling can be wonderful. A teenager who has felt misunderstood and alone in the family may suddenly have a new family member close to his or her own age to talk to and confide in. Many stepsiblings go on to form strong, lifelong bonds.

Becoming a healthy family when there are stepparents and stepsiblings involved takes a lot of time and effort on everyone's part. You'll learn more about remarriage and the issues that can arise around stepfamilies in Chapter Three.

When a Sibling Has Special Needs

The phrase *special needs* refers to the extra care required by a person who is ill or disabled in some way. These conditions may range from mild learning disabilities to serious chronic illnesses, such as muscular dystrophy; conditions caused by chromosomal abnormalities, such as Down's syndrome; and physical disabilities, such as blindness or cerebral palsy. The extra care that a person with special needs may require includes special tutoring or, depending on the severity of the illness or disability, assistance with every aspect of daily life.

People who have a brother or sister with special needs become extremely familiar with their sibling's condition and care. The extra attention and cost involved usually become a regular part of the family routine. If you do have a special-needs sibling you may have learned some valuable skills, such as reading Braille or speaking in sign language. Or you may simply have discovered, through early experience, the values of care, patience, and compassion. What you no doubt know is that first and foremost, your sibling is your sibling—sometimes a friend, sometimes a major annoyance. Sometimes, though, you may find yourself having concerns and feelings that arise as the result of your sibling's condition. Donald J. Meyer, the founder of the Sibling Support Project, a national support program for young people whose siblings have special needs, cowrote a book entitled *Sibshops: Workshops for Brothers and Sisters of*

Children with Special Needs. According to Meyer, people in this situation may experience some or all of the following emotions.

- **Overidentification.** At times a young person may worry that he or she may develop his or her sibling's condition.
- **Embarrassment.** No matter how accustomed a teen is to a sibling's condition, it may embarrass him or her in some way, particularly when the family is out in public.
- **Guilt.** Young people may feel bad about the occasional negative feelings they have toward disabled or ill siblings, including embarrassment or resentment over how much parental time and attention their brother's or sister's disability demands.
- **Isolation, loneliness, and loss.** Some young people may miss having a fully functioning sibling like their friends have. These feelings can be especially intense if the brother or sister was once well and has recently become ill. In addition, the fact that parents must spend so much time caring and attending to the needs of an ill or disabled sibling often magnifies these feelings of loneliness and isolation.
- **Concerns for the future.** Many teenagers may wonder what will happen once their parents are no longer able to care for their sibling. They may especially worry that the burden of care may someday fall on their shoulders.
- **Increased responsibility.** People with siblings who have special needs often take on additional responsibilities and chores, from cooking to handling finances. This usually occurs because the burdens of caring for the child with special needs leave the parents too busy and exhausted to do these things themselves.
- **Pressure to achieve.** Sometimes those who have a sibling with special needs put themselves under intense pressure to behave perfectly or excel in school, sports,

or other activities. This feeling may sometimes come from the parents, but it also may arise from an urgency on the young person's part to get attention or to compensate for the sibling's inability to satisfy perceived parental hopes.

These are all normal feelings and concerns. Like all issues faced by all families, the best way to handle them is through direct, effective communication within the family. Talking with other teens who have siblings with special needs can also help. If you have a sibling with special needs, see Chapter Six for a listing of places you can contact to help you cope with these issues.

Issues in Mixed-Race Families

As you learned in the last chapter, there are an increasing number of families composed of people from different racial, religious, and cultural backgrounds. Many teenagers today have biological parents of different racial backgrounds, making them biracial or multiracial.

Like all families, mixed-race families can be healthy. And as with all types of families, the key to a healthy family lies in the way the members treat one another—with love, compassion, and respect, and through constant and effective communication. In addition, mixed-race families do have a unique set of issues and gratifications. Being part of a mixed-race family can teach young children the lesson that the quality of a person lies not in that person's color and creed but in his or her values and priorities. In other words, it's what's inside that counts. And coming from more than one culture exposes young people to the different styles and customs that humans from different parts of the world may experience.

On the other hand, children who grow up in mixed-race families sometimes face a basic question of identity: Where do I fit? Their parents and caregivers may have consciously pushed them to identify one way or another—as an African American, if one parent was black and the other was white, for example. Or they may have tried to instill a strong sense of belonging to more than one race and culture.

In *Black, White, Other: Biracial Americans Talk About Race and Identity,* author Lise Funderburg, herself a biracial person, talked with others about their experiences of race and identity. Parental and family influence was important, as was the way the outside world viewed them. If they were generally viewed as being a person of a certain ethnic group, they were more likely to identify with that part of their culture than with the other. If one side of their extended family was more involved in and accepting of their upbringing, it made a difference too. Some people reported identifying with one aspect of their heritage publicly and with another, or both, privately. In the end, racial identification is an intensely personal experience. It will be equally so for teenagers who come from families of different religious and cultural origins.

Adoption

Most teenagers begin the process of developing a sense of their own identity around age 11 or 12. The natural question surrounding this phase is, "Who am I?" For many young people, discovering the answer to this question means exploring where they come from—looking at how they are similar to or different from their parents and siblings and developing a sense of family history. When a child has been adopted, it's very natural that he or she will begin to become curious about his or her biological parents at this time.

Many health professionals assumed at one time that this part of identity development was extremely difficult and painful for adopted teenagers; after all, this theory said, it would underscore the fact that these teenagers were not originally from the family they had grown up with. In addition, it would raise questions about what type of people the biological parents were, and why they did not want their natural child. The answers for teenagers who did decide to pursue their biological origins were often hard to find. Until recently, most adoptions were "closed," meaning that neither the child nor the adoptive parents knew much about the birth parents. Many children did not have access to specific information regarding their biological parents' ages, medical histories, and cultural or ethnic backgrounds.

Then, in 1994, a study funded by the National Institute of Mental Health and conducted by the Search Institute found that teenagers growing up in healthy, adoptive families were not plagued by identity problems. The study surveyed 715 families with teenagers who were adopted as infants, and it included mixed-race adoptions. For most of the teens surveyed, adoption did not negatively affect their mental health or identity development. Most of them had strong emotional bonds with their adoptive parents. And most of the families dealt with the adoption as an accepted fact. It wasn't dwelt on, but these families did discuss the subject freely and openly, according to the researchers.

Even so, there are some issues that many adopted children face during their teenage years. Some young people may find themselves grieving to a certain extent the loss of the birth family and their cultural background, and some teenagers may experience a feeling of stigma over being adopted. Most teenagers distance themselves from their families to some extent during adolescence. In doing so, adoptive teens may fantasize about their birth families. They may find themselves wondering, for example, whether they had biological siblings, or whether their natural parents would have placed the same rules and limitations on them as their adoptive family has.

In general, it is not uncommon for teenagers to wonder why they were placed for adoption. And some experience feelings of rejection by their birth parents. According to the Search Institute study, however, few teenagers growing up in healthy families experience a loss of self-esteem as a result of their normal curiosity.

Healthy families deal with the issue of adoption in different ways. All of them most likely talk openly about it with their children, although some parents may or may not choose to share information they may have regarding their adopted children's origins. Teenagers who decide to search for their biological parents often find the process extremely emotional and time-consuming, as are actual reunions. Both require a high level of emotional maturity. Since adolescence is itself an emotional roller coaster at times, many adoptive parents—with the support of many adoption experts—may urge these teenagers to postpone such a meeting until they are adults.

Transracial and Transcultural Adoptions

For teenagers who were adopted transracially or transculturally, like Ira, reconciling their two different ethnic or racial backgrounds is part of the process of identity formation. In exploring the question "Who am I?" they may also ask, "Where do I belong?" and "What does it mean to be a different color from my family?" These are important questions. Young children often pay little attention to skin color and consider everyone a potential playmate, but in junior and senior high school, teenagers have a tendency to form social groups and cliques that are often based on or associated with race or cultural background. Teenagers who straddle two groups may find themselves in a difficult position. They also may face questions of racism, a sad fact of today's society.

Healthy families who have adopted transracially or transculturally are aware of the issues their adopted children may have to face. They know that eventually their children may have to deal with issues of race and prejudice, experiences that the rest of the family may not encounter. Healthy families help their children find ways to cope with these issues and work hard to build self-esteem so that these young people are strong enough to handle them and prosper. They listen and do not minimize racial questions and concerns.

Ira's parents have tried to address some of these issues in the course of their everyday lives. In addition to joining the club of other families with transracially adopted kids, they have always lived in integrated neighborhoods. They also make a point of exposing all their children to various aspects of black culture, taking them to plays, concerts, and other cultural events. Ira's brother, Mike, boasts that he knows more black-history trivia than any other white guy in the world.

The National Adoption Information Clearinghouse, a branch of the U.S. Department of Health and Human Services, emphasizes the importance of identity issues for transracially adopted children. They offer these suggestions to families to help give their children a sense of cultural identity as well as a strong connection with their adoptive families.

- Do not tolerate racially or ethnically biased remarks. Counter them, and teach the child how to reply to them, clearly and graciously, without starting a fight.
- Develop a supportive network of family and friends.
- Celebrate all cultures.
- Make race and culture an open topic of discussion. Talk about racial issues and the ways different people are treated differently.
- Expose the child to a variety of experiences that will enhance the child's physical and intellectual skills and in that way build self-esteem.
- Take the child to places where most of the people present are from his or her race or ethnic group. This

may include a trip back to the country of origin if it was an overseas adoption.

- Emphasize the way the child fits into the adoptive family, by stressing, for example, the interests family members share.
- Offer strong positive role models to help young people feel proud of their racial or cultural heritage.

The love and support young people receive in healthy families will help them greatly in developing a healthy self-image. That, as well as the interpersonal skills that they learn relating to respect, communicating effectively, and resolving conflicts, will be particularly helpful in situations of family stress. You will learn about these periods in chapter 3.

3

Family Stress

Something really terrible has happened—Eli's grandfather has died, very suddenly. Eli doesn't know how to handle it. No one he's been close to has ever died before. His mother is being very strong about it. Eli has barely seen her cry, except briefly at Bud's funeral. He wishes he could be that strong, but the truth is, Eli finds himself close to tears whenever he thinks about his grandfather. Eli really misses him; he could talk to Bud about anything.

Eli's mother has just announced that she's selling his grandfather's house. "He's gone, Eli," she said when he protested. "Holding on to the house isn't going to bring him back. We can use the money, and we need to get on with our lives." Easier said than done, Eli thinks to himself. He knows that his mother is as sad as he is about his grandfather's death and that she's trying to be strong for Eli's sake. But how is he going to go on without Bud?

Shira has noticed that Rick is moodier than ever these days. She's heard him yelling at her mother almost every night over the past couple of weeks, and she knows he's been drinking. There are empty beer bottles all over the house. Yesterday Shira finally asked her mother if something's going on with him. Shira's mother told her that Rick had recently been laid off from his job but didn't want anyone to know. "That's why he's been so crabby, Shira. He's really upset and hurt over what happened to him at the plant." Shira thinks that Rick has every right to be upset about losing his job. She just doesn't like the fact that he's been taking it out on her mother.

Ira's family moved to the Midwest from the West Coast over the Christmas break. His mother was transferred. She's a bank executive and got a promotion that she said she couldn't refuse. Ira is happy for her, but misses the beach, his old school, and most of all, his friends. Here, he's a bit self-conscious. Black kids and white kids don't seem to mix much, yet he's a black kid with a white family. Where does he fit in?

Yesterday Ira passed his older brother, Mike, in the hall between classes. "Meet me out front after school and I'll give you a ride home," Mike called. Simple enough, but a kid from Ira's biology class, a black guy Ira's never spoken to, fell into step with Ira and asked, "Who was that?" "My brother," Ira said. "No way," came the response. "Yeah." Ira shrugged. But inside he was ticked off. "Man," he thought, "why should I have to explain my family to a total stranger?"

For whatever reason, Marcy had been clinging to the hope that her parents would somehow work things out and stay together. Now she knows it will never happen, because her dad has moved out and has told both Marcy and Ben that he and their mother are going to get a divorce. Of course they could never get back together, she tells herself all the time. Look at how unhappy they were. She also thinks about how nervous and upset their constant arguments made her. Even so, Marcy's in pain about it.

She'd really like to talk to Ben, but she can't. He's like a completely different person these days. And he's got his own problems; he was caught smoking pot near the shopping mall last week by the police. Marcy's parents had to go with him to court, and she's sure they spent the whole time fighting with each other and blaming the other for Ben's problems.

Annie has been there for Marcy during some really rough times lately. Listening to her friend, Annie's grateful that her parents didn't fight like that when they split up five years ago. That doesn't mean the divorce was easy for her and Lisa. At first they really missed seeing their father every day. They got used to it, though. They see him several times each week. The hardest thing for Annie and Lisa came a few years after the divorce, when their parents started dating other people. Their father's new girlfriend was OK—nothing special, but OK. But when they found out their mother was involved with a woman, it was really hard on both girls.

At one time or another, most families experience a major change in their lives. This change can be a good one, as is the case with Ira's family, who moved because his mother has a great new job, or a tragic one, such as the death of Eli's grandfather. Any type of change, however, causes a family to go through a transition of some sort, which almost always leads to stress.

Family stress affects all members of the family in one way or another. At times a stressful situation can bring family members closer. Annie and Lisa, for example, became very tight after their parents separated. There are times, though, that stress can pull a family apart, at least temporarily. No matter how healthy and communicative a family is, surviving family stress can be challenging. But with patience, work, and some luck, it can be done.

Coping with Loss

One of the first and most important things to know about events that cause family stress is that they often involve some sort of a loss. Of course the death of a loved one is the most profound cause of loss, but the cause could also be the loss of a job or business, a move that involves the loss of a supportive group of friends, or a divorce and the frequent loss of daily contact with one parent. When people experience a major loss, such as the one Eli suffered with the death of his grandfather, they almost always go through a period of grief and mourning.

Grief is the emotional reaction one has to a loss. It can involve feelings of sadness, helplessness, confusion, and anger. The intensity of these emotions will vary depending on the type of loss involved and whether it was expected or came suddenly. Elisabeth Kübler-Ross, an expert on death and dying, identified a process a person goes through while grieving. Although Kübler-Ross conceived her model for those coping with the death of a loved one or one's own terminal illness, it is a process that applies to any type of loss, such as those brought on by a move or a divorce.

As he grieves for his grandfather, Eli is likely to go through the following stages:

1. **Shock and denial.** During the first stage of the grieving process Eli keeps telling himself that there's no way Bud has died—it must be a dream or a joke or something, but Bud could not possibly be dead.
2. **Anger.** Eli now believes that Bud is really gone, and he's angry about it. He may take his anger out on his mother or close friends, and he may express his anger verbally or physically, punching walls or slamming doors. He may also at times turn his anger inward. "If I were a better grandson to him," he may think, "he

wouldn't have left me like this." Anger turned inward is known as guilt.

3. **Bargaining.** Eli is starting to think in ways he's never thought before. "Tell you what," he finds himself saying to God. "You bring Bud back, and I'll be the best person around. I'll work for the poor, feed the hungry, you name it. But do this one thing for me." As strange as that may sound, bargaining is a very common and natural stage in the grieving process.

4. **Depression.** The bargaining is over, and Eli knows Bud isn't coming back. He's beginning to feel profound sadness as he comes to realize that there was nothing he could do to prevent Bud from dying, and nothing he can do now to bring him back.

5. **Acceptance.** Eli will eventually work through his shock, anger, and sadness and will learn to accept the change in his life. It may take him awhile, and he'll always miss Bud terribly. But he will be able to make peace with himself and with his grandfather and go on with his life.

Whether a person is grieving the loss of a loved one, or the losses brought on by other changes, it's important to remember that the process of grieving takes time. If you are coping with a loss, keep in mind that you will experience a host of powerful emotions that can be overwhelming. But it helps to recognize what those emotions are and to let yourself feel them.

It also helps to do something constructive to help yourself along. Try getting involved in an activity you enjoy but have never done before, or finding a new hobby that keeps you busy. At the same time, be sure to take care of yourself: Eat properly, exercise, and get lots of sleep. Some people find that keeping a journal and writing about their feelings helps. And it's always a good idea to be honest and open about those feelings. Maybe there are friends or trusted adults you can talk to about them. And allow yourself to cry when you have to. It's an honest response to a painful experience, and it can make you feel better.

If you are in so much pain that you don't think there's any way out of it, and you find yourself doing things that can be harmful, such as taking drugs or drinking, be sure to find help for yourself. Think about calling an adult you know, such as a teacher or coach, a school counselor, your family doctor, or your spiritual leader. There are also youth crisis helplines that you can contact. They can put you in touch with a peer support group where you could connect with kids in similar situations to your own. It is often very helpful to talk with others who understand from personal experience exactly what you are going through and how you are feeling. For more information on contacting these support groups, see chapter 6.

Moves

According to a 1996 report from the U.S. Census Bureau, 17 percent of American families move homes every year. More than 9 million children are uprooted in the process. They often leave behind close friends, extended family members, and familiar schools and neighborhoods.

For Ira, leaving his friends behind has been by far the hardest part about moving. He had a lot of buddies in his old school and was really close to Jordan and Kyle, whom he'd known since the second grade. Now, in a completely new place, Ira suddenly feels shy and self-conscious. Everyone in his class goes way back with one another, and they have a shared history he can't be any part of. And to make things more difficult, there are more racial tensions in his new school than there were in his old one. Black kids tend to stick together, apart from the white kids, and the few Hispanics in his school don't really talk to anyone but one another. In his old school everyone just sort of hung out together. The whole move has left Ira lonely and more confused than ever about his identity.

Ira's lucky. He can talk about what's going on at school with his folks. His father pointed out that there wasn't much he could do about the racial divide, but he reminded Ira that it takes only a couple of new friends to help you feel at home. He suggested that Ira find a club he wants to join—Ira had always been involved in drama at his old school. At least then he'd have a sense of belonging.

Ira has particular issues he has to cope with in getting used to his move, but the truth is that adjusting to a new social situation is always hard. Trying to make friends and meet new people involves a level of risk—the risk of rejection. During adolescence, when friendships become extremely important, the fear of rejection is particularly great. Moves are especially difficult for young people who have trouble making friends, perhaps as a result of shyness or low self-esteem. Some schools have set up tutoring and "buddy" systems in these situations. In addition to giving students the extra academic help they need, the new students are introduced around the school by a classmate, often one who has "survived" a move him- or herself. A "buddy" showed Ira around in his new school, and the guy has become a friend, kind of.

One thing Ira's dad reminded him is that the move could have been much more traumatic—it could have been for a tragic reason. It's true that the most difficult moves to cope with are the ones that come as the result of a family crisis, such as a death, divorce, or financial setback. Young people in these situations have to cope not only with the pain of moving itself but often with the loss of support systems within the family as well.

These types of moves are traumatic for all family members, but they are often particularly hard on teenagers, who unlike younger children, can fully understand and grieve about the reasons for the move. And there are times that parents are just as upset over the situation as their children are. When parents are depressed, they can't always offer their children the support they need, particularly during a change. Sometimes the roles actually reverse, and the teenager ends up supporting and taking care of the parent. To some extent, this is what is happening to Marcy.

Divorce

Since her parents split up, Marcy has lived with her mother. But lately Marcy has felt like *she's* really the one in charge. When her parents aren't fighting, her mother cries a lot, sometimes staying in her bedroom all day. Marcy does all of the cleaning around the house and most of the cooking. If she doesn't do it, they order pizza. It's a drag, but Marcy thinks she can handle it—for a while. Marcy's less sure of how to respond when her mother confides in her, as she did last night. "I'm so scared, Marcy. What am I going to do?" Marcy feels scared too.

Divorce is tough on everyone in the family. The stress unfolds over a long period of time. A divorce usually follows a lot of unhappiness and conflict between a couple: They may have tried to work out their differences through counseling or living apart for a time and found ultimately that they couldn't. With the decision to divorce, the existing family structure is shattered. Family members have to find new ways of relating to one another. Although Annie's parents have managed it, it is often easier said than done.

A divorce can bring up many issues. Teenagers may be scared about family finances and their future—who will pay for college? Sometimes a divorced couple may end up living in different states. This means that the children involved will have to cope both with the loss of a parent and the upheaval of relocation in addition to the stress of the divorce itself.

For children and teenagers, the emotions involved in a divorce can be complex and confusing. They are likely to feel both sadness about and anger toward their parents. They may also feel guilty about the breakup, like it was somehow their fault. Marcy sometimes has thoughts such as the following: "Dad wouldn't have left if he really loved me, so I must not be lovable, right?" It's important to note that teenagers and children are never to blame for their parents' divorce.

It's not surprising that many children and teenagers who have experienced a divorce suffer a loss of confidence. Teenagers and younger kids need a lot of guidance from their parents to help them sort out some of these emotions. The problem, of course, is that sometimes parents may be too distracted by their own feelings surrounding the divorce to be of much help to their children.

This is particularly true if the decision to divorce is not a mutual one. If, let's say, a husband does not want to split up but his wife does, the husband could become so wrapped up in his own feelings that he either neglects his children or leans heavily on them for his own emotional support.

The Damage Done

Fortunately, long-term studies of divorced families show that—except in extreme cases—the adults do get their lives back on track, usually within three years following the divorce. Teenagers, however, aren't always so lucky.

Some studies indicate that teenagers whose parents have divorced are more likely to develop academic or drug problems, drop out of school, or become pregnant than are young people whose parents are still together. Certain experts blame divorce itself. If more parents worked on keeping their marriages intact, their children wouldn't have these problems. Many other researchers say that the greatest harm to children and teens comes from living in homes where the parents don't get along. It is the predivorce fighting, they say, that does the most damage.

One point all experts do agree on is that the way in which the parents handle the divorce itself, and their relationship afterward, is crucial to their children's adjustment. If the divorcing parents are always fighting or are so caught up in their own anger and sadness that they ignore their children's needs for attention and discipline, there's a good chance that there will be problems. This could be what's happening in Marcy's family. Marcy feels alternately "invisible" or inappropriately in charge. Her brother Ben is just tuning out and turning to drugs.

Abandonment

After a divorce, one parent will usually stay with the children, while the other one moves out. The parent who no longer lives in the family home following a divorce is called the "noncustodial" parent. Ideally, that parent should have a lot of regular contact with his or her children—daily, weekly, or for longer periods of time during school breaks. In general, it's important for teenagers and younger children to stay closely connected to both parents following a divorce, except in cases where contact would expose them to violence and abuse.

It sometimes happens, though, that noncustodial parents begin missing or avoiding visits with their children. Sometimes they disappear altogether. When that happens, it is called "abandonment." Young people whose parents abandon them in this way have every right to feel angry. Many blame themselves for being unlovable, just as they did when their parents split up. It's important, once again, to remember that teenagers and children are never to blame for their parents' problems. Parents who abandon their sons and daughters are not driven to it by their children but are acting on their own selfish or troubled instincts.

Nevertheless, abandonment can be devastating to a teenager's self-esteem. The best thing a teenager who has been abandoned can do is to seek help by speaking to a trusted adult or to a counselor. Eventually, there are ways to heal the damage caused by abandonment. Some teens are able to do so by finding mentors or role models to guide them. For more information on role models and mentors, see Chapter Five.

Taking Control

If, like Marcy, you are coping with your parents' divorce, there are some steps you can take to help you gain some control of the situation. Here are three strategies that can get you started.

1. Talk to your parents about what you're feeling. Of course, this isn't always easy. It could be that you don't want to burden your parents with your own problems. Marcy certainly feels that way, particularly around her mother. If it makes it easier for you, you might want to try role-playing by trying out what you plan to say with a friend.

    It's also a good idea to stick to the effective communication techniques you learned in Chapter 2. In particular, try to use as many "I" messages as possible so that you don't put your parents on the defensive.

    Marcy, for example, could clearly say to each of her parents, "When you fight and make threats in front of me, I feel sad and scared. I feel like I'm being asked to take sides. I love you both and don't want to do that." She could tell her mother that she feels worried about her mom's constant sadness and suggest that she see a doctor.

    You may be nervous speaking to your parents about this, and it is completely understandable if you are. Keep in mind, though, that your parents will probably be grateful to you for telling them exactly how you feel. You are extremely important to them, even if it doesn't always seem that way. They are just going through tough times and have tuned out what is going on around them.

    It may seem that this is basic advice without much scientific backup, but in fact, one study cited by

Stephanie Coontz in her 1997 book *The Way We Really Are* shows that communicating with parents does help to ease tensions. In the study, children filled out questionnaires that asked how they felt about their parents' treatment of each other. The researchers then sent the information to their divorced parents. Those parents, they found, cut back significantly on their fighting. Listening to how you feel about what's going on may well jar your parents out of their own worlds and onto a healing track.

2. Talk to a counselor. A counselor can help you sort out your feelings and give you positive direction. If you're finding it hard to confront your parents directly, the counselor will call them in and help you make your point clear to them. Your problems and emotions, not your parents' strong feelings toward each other, will be the focus of the discussion. They will be forced to listen.

3. Find a support group. While it is easy to feel alone in this situation, you aren't. Divorce is so common that there are many teenagers who are going through the exact same process as you. A counselor can help you find an appropriate group. (See Chapter Six for a list of available resources.)

New Relationships and Blended Families

When Annie's father first introduced her to his new girl-friend, Annie was happy for him—in a way. Her parents had been living apart for a couple of years, and Annie suspected that her dad was lonely. She just wasn't sure whether Susan was right for him. Susan seemed a bit uptight. She was always perfectly dressed, without a hair out of place, whereas Annie's dad always wears casual things, jeans and denim work shirts. And Susan has a son. Billy was eight when Annie first met Susan. Annie found herself wondering what would happen if her father married Susan. Would Billy take up all of his time?

Parents often form new relationships at some point following a divorce or the death of their first partner. As you learned in chapter 1, when a person who has at least one child remarries or moves in with someone, a blended family forms. This can be stressful for everyone involved—and there can be a lot of people involved.

As you know by now, young people in this situation may find themselves with one or more stepparents, new adults in their lives who expect to have some authority over them. They may have one or two sets of stepsiblings. They may even find their positions in these blended families different—an oldest child may now be in the middle. And there are new extended families to deal with—grandparents, aunts, uncles, cousins.

For teenagers who have already had to cope with the loss of their "first" family, the prospect of a remarriage may open old wounds. They may worry about being abandoned by their parents, replaced in their affections by the new partner or stepchildren. They may also feel renewed guilt, anger, and sadness over a parent's death or their parents' divorce.

Another problem that teenagers in new blended families sometimes encounter is that they often have to behave in a way that is not necessarily natural to them at that time in their life. Adolescents, as some experts point out, normally pull away from their families to some extent. But teens who are in blended families are often pressured to spend a lot of time with the "new" family—a demand some teenagers resent and have difficulty in delivering.

In addition, many teenagers who join blended families find themselves caught between the needs of two other family members. When this occurs, a loyalty conflict can result. A teenager may experience a loyalty conflict, for instance, if she likes her new stepmother, but her biological mother resents her ex-husband's remarriage. The teen may feel bad about showing any affection for the stepmother for fear of hurting her mother. A father may experience a loyalty conflict when his new wife tries to discipline his teenager and the teen ignores her, saying "You can't do anything to me. You aren't my mother."

It takes time to get used to being in a new family, but most teenagers do make the adjustment. In the meantime, there are some ways to reduce the initial stress. If you are having trouble adjusting to a blended family, you may want to think about the following.

- Try to understand why your parents are finding new relationships and thinking of remarriage. They aren't doing it to hurt you but to get on with their life after going through hard times. If you make an effort to see things from their side, it may help give you some perspective.
- Try to avoid causing loyalty conflicts for your parent. It's not unusual for a teenager to have some difficulty communicating with a stepparent, at least at first. But should a conflict arise, try not to put your father or mother in the middle of the dispute. It will only make everyone feel bad. When disputes arise, try using the conflict resolution skills outlined in chapter 2.
- Practice effective communication—with parents, stepparents, and stepsiblings. Try to really listen to what is being said. If you have concerns, try to use "I" messages when voicing them.
- Aim for mutual respect. You don't have to be best friends with the new members of your family—especially not at first—but you should respect them, and they you. Experts advise new stepparents to make mutual respect their first goal with their stepchildren. Mutual respect should be your goal as well. Friendship and affection may follow.
- If the remarriage has forced you and your family to move, you will feel a real sense of loss, as you learned earlier in this chapter. Expect to grieve.

- If you just can't overcome your anger, sense of loss, or settle into your new situation, talk to a counselor. Being part of a blended family carries unique challenges that can be hard to deal with alone, and you shouldn't have to. There are people you can go to who will help you.

Family Counseling

When Ben's parents accompanied him to court following his arrest for possession of marijuana, the judge told them that their fighting was part of Ben's problem. Ben needs supervision and limits, the judge said, and he can't get it from parents who are distracted by their own marital problems. Ben was placed on probation and ordered to get drug counseling. Marcy's parents were told to get family counseling. Counseling, the judge said, would help them find a way to work together as parents, if not as married partners.

Read any book—including this one—about being a teenager and you'll find a lot of discussion about the importance of speaking to a counselor when a given problem is too great to be handled alone. There are different types of counseling. Therapists may specialize in treating women, men, married couples, teenagers, or children. A family therapist is a trained professional (usually a psychologist, psychiatrist, social worker, or member of the clergy) who treats families, both on an individual basis and as a group.

Family counseling is appropriate in any stressful situation, ranging from a child's behavioral problem, eating disorder, or drug or alcohol problem, to chronic family fighting and the stress surrounding a divorce and/or remarriage. Family therapy helps families work out their problems—together.

Family therapists differ in approach, but in general they give everyone in the family an opportunity to talk about a difficult situation and make sure those opinions are heard and understood by the other family members. Therapists guide discussions among family members by asking questions and encouraging everyone to ask each other questions and to listen actively to their answers. If emotions during these discussions threaten to get out control, the therapist will step in and attempt to calm things down. The therapist will also suggest constructive ways for the family to communicate and handle difficult situations that arise on a day-to-day basis.

Family therapy usually takes a period of weeks or months. Sometimes the whole family will attend sessions with the therapist. At other times, the individual family members will have private meetings with the counselor. Everything said at these meetings is confidential. A therapist will not tell a parent anything that a teenager has said in a private session without the teen's consent. The only times that rule will be broken is if a therapist suspects that a child is the victim of abuse or that someone's life may be in danger. In those cases, the therapist is legally required to notify the proper authorities.

Ben, Marcy, and their parents attend family therapy sessions once a week. So far everyone's been really quiet, but the therapist is working hard to get them all to open up. She's told Ben and Marcy that they can say anything they want about their parents' divorce and their behavior surrounding the divorce. The therapist will make sure the parents are listening by asking them specific questions about what their son and daughter are saying.

Likewise, Ben's parents will have a chance to express their feelings and concerns about his drug use, as will Marcy. She thinks he acts like a jerk toward her when he's high but isn't sure she's going to be able to actually say that. The therapist has told the family that it's really important for them to be up-front and honest. Once she knows the way everyone is feeling, the therapist will suggest ways their parents can work through their emotions toward each other. She will get them past the urge to simply blame each other for family problems.

Homosexuality and the Family

Annie's family has gone through family therapy too, but unlike Marcy and Ben, who were referred to a counselor through a judge, it was Annie's mother who suggested that everyone go to a counselor. She thought her daughters might need help understanding what it meant to have a mother who is a lesbian. She was right.

They will never forget the night they found out. Annie was 13, and Lisa was 11. Their mom took them away for the weekend to a cabin she'd rented at a nearby lake. The second night they were there, she waited until after dinner and then told them that she had something important and "kind of complicated" that she had to tell them. Quietly and calmly, their mother explained that she was in love with a woman, her friend Lin, whom the girls had met a few times. She said that her feelings for Lin had surprised even her. At first, she had refused to acknowledge them. When the feelings didn't go away, though, she said she had to accept them. She realized that she was a lesbian, a woman who is sexually attracted to other women. She hoped that someday Lin would become her "life partner"; it would be sort of like they were married. But she wanted the girls to get used to the idea first.

Annie and Lisa were surprised and confused. They didn't really understand what a lesbian was. They sort of thought it was something dirty and bad. Annie remembers feeling really angry with her mother. She barely spoke to her for three days. School was about to begin. What if the kids at school found out and teased her? Did they even have to know? And Annie wondered if she was a lesbian too. Was it something that you inherited from your parents, like blue eyes or brown hair?

Fortunately for the girls, their mother had anticipated that they would be incredibly confused and upset, and she was ready to deal with it. She knew her daughters' reaction would be the hardest part of her "coming out," which is what it's called when someone announces to friends or family members that he or she is gay, lesbian, or bisexual. Annie and Lisa's mother found the girls some books about children who have homosexual parents. She also took them to see a family therapist.

The therapy sessions helped Annie and Lisa understand more about why their mother made the choices she did. As important, they helped them accept those choices and to realize that regardless of whom she was with, their mother was and always would be a wonderful, loving parent to the two of them. Annie and Lisa's father attended a couple of the sessions, and he, too, learned to deal with his ex-wife's decision. At one point he told the girls, in front of their mother, that they were welcome to live with him if they chose to. It was nice to hear, but both girls decided to stay with their mom.

It seems like that all happened a long time ago. Now Lin lives with them, and Annie likes her. She's smart and funny. She seems to make their mother happy. Annie has told some close friends, such as Marcy, about her mom, and they've been OK with it. But she's careful about whom she tells and whom she brings home. It's good to be cautious.

Homosexual Parents

It is generally estimated that as many as 1 in 10 people are homosexual. This estimate would mean that there are around 24 million homosexuals in the United States. Some have chosen to come out and live their lifestyle openly, whereas others choose either not to act on their feelings or not to tell those they are close to that they have.

It's important for some people to know that the children of lesbian, gay, and bisexual parents are as likely to be "straight" when they grow up as are those with heterosexual parents. In other words, the fact that Annie's mother is a lesbian does not mean that Annie will also be one. Nobody knows exactly what makes some people heterosexual and others homosexual.

According to the American Psychological Association, many scientists believe that sexual orientation is determined for most people early in life, through a combination of "biological, psychological, and social factors." It isn't simply passed from parent to child genetically or through exposure to the parent's homosexuality. Most important, homosexuality is not a mental illness or an emotional problem, and it is not a matter of choice. Most people cannot voluntarily change their sexual orientation.

Can lesbians and gay men be good parents? Yes, according to existing studies that compare children raised by gay parents and by straight parents. These studies indicate that there are no major differences between the children based on the parent's sexual orientation. Young people with homosexual parents can be just as bright, popular, and well adjusted as any other teenagers.

One situation that can cause problems for the children of a homosexual parent, however, is if there is a bitter divorce or custody fight—a situation that can be just as damaging for the children of heterosexual parents. In the case of a child with a gay parent, this is particularly true if the mother or father loses visitation rights.

Teenagers who have homosexual parents and are looking for a support network, can get in touch with COLAGE (Children Of Lesbians And Gays Everywhere). Based in San Francisco, COLAGE has chapters all over the country. COLAGE's mailing and web site addresses are listed in Chapter Six.

When a Child Comes Out

Having a parent come out is likely to disrupt the whole family, at least temporarily. It raises questions and concerns for the children and the other parent that have to be addressed. Likewise, when a child announces that he or she is homosexual or bisexual, it also affects the rest of the family. Coming out requires careful planning and clear communication. If you are considering taking this step, be sure to consider the following strategies.

- Think about what you want to say and how you want to say it very carefully. Role-play, if necessary.
- Carefully choose when and where to make your announcement.
- Remind your family members that you love them and are still the same person.
- Give them time to absorb the news. You probably spent a lot of time coming to terms with your sexual orientation and deciding to come out. Be prepared for others to need the same time, even if their initial reaction is negative.
- Have a support system in place for yourself—trusted friends, a counselor, a support network of other gay and lesbian youth (see Chapter Six for contact information).
- Be prepared to guide your family members to sources of reliable information on homosexuality and possibly to support networks for parents, friends, and family members of lesbians and gays, such as Parents and Friends of Lesbians and Gays, or PFLAG (see Chapter Six for contact information). They may not know that such resources exist.

What Other People Think

A lot of people hide their homosexuality from their families, and even from themselves, because they worry about how other people will react. In fact, what other people think is a very real source of stress for today's families and for their individual members. As you learned earlier in this chapter, many of today's families challenge old ideas about how families should look and function. It is only recently that racially mixed families—through marriage, birth, or adoption—have become common. Interracial marriage was even illegal in 16 states before 1967. Religiously mixed families are also a reasonably new phenomenon. In recent years, for example, the number of marriages between Jews and Christians has skyrocketed, resulting in many families that practice two faiths under one roof.

Stress for members of nontraditional families can be both external and internal. Ira, for instance, experiences a bit of both types of stress. He isn't comfortable explaining to new acquaintances how he has come to be a black teenager in a white family. He doesn't think he should have to. At the same time, it's not always easy for him to tune out the disapproval that he often suspects is behind the curiosity. In addition, he's just starting to comprehend the issues of racial identification that he faces. Over the years, his parents have also had to deal with intrusive questions about Ira's birth and adoption, as well as more serious questions about whether or not white parents can raise a black child with any sense of racial identity.

A religiously mixed family can experience a clash of cultures within the family. People of different faiths are often raised in ignorance of each other's holidays and customs. The resulting confusion can sometimes be misinterpreted as insensitivity. Members of the extended family, such as grandparents, may feel that their beliefs and customs have been rejected in these mixed families and put pressure on the mixed family in that way. Teenagers may feel tugged at both ends to choose the practice of one religion over another. This may also be true for children in ethic and culturally mixed families, where children may, for instance, choose one language over another.

Finally, something going on in a teenager's life can trigger a feeling of shame for the rest of the family. People care what others think of them. If their children get into some sort of trouble, such as delinquency, teen pregnancy, or drug use, parents and caregivers may feel that they will be blamed or shamed by *their* peers. In some cases, that alone may spark a family crisis.

Resolving these issues is tough—and very personal. In some cases, it may be best to ignore other people's objections and questions, which is what Ira's parents did when they decided to bring Ira into their family. Doing this requires a high level of confidence and self-esteem, but interestingly enough, taking this path can actually work to boost a person's sense of confidence. Being able to act with integrity in spite of other people's fears and prejudices can be very freeing.

There are also times, however, when the pressures and opinions are too great or upsetting to overcome or ignore. When this happens, the best thing to do is to accept help and guidance from another person, be it a family member, close friend, or trusted adult.

One of the best outcomes of the very different look and composition of today's families is the emergence of support and discussion groups for families, adults, and teenagers in almost every area. If you need help contacting such a group, talk to a school counselor. And remember that times are changing. In spite of the enormous strain that a divorce puts on a family, for instance, its sheer prevalence means that it no longer carries the social stigma it once did. "Official" forms of discrimination—laws and policies—are rapidly disappearing. Public opinion will eventually follow.

If you are in the middle of a stressful situation, it may feel as though time has stopped. You may wonder if the pain will ever go away, or if your family life will always be this painful and confusing. Keep in mind, though, that with time and proper action, many types of family stress can be resolved effectively and constructively. And it could be that the stress itself has some surprisingly redeeming factors. You may find that both you and your family are stronger for having gone through the experience.

4

Coping with Dysfunction

Shira is unbelievably angry and deeply upset. Rick hit her mother last night. He was drunk. This morning, when he was sober and hung over, he saw her mother's black eye and said he was sorry, that it would never happen again. But Shira worries that it will. She's heard Rick yell at and threaten her mother before. These days Shira's mom spends a lot of time tiptoeing around Rick; she doesn't want to do or say anything that might upset him, especially when he's had a few drinks. She makes excuses for him, too, saying that he's just under stress.

Shira's angry with Rick for having hit her mom, but she's mad at her mother too. "Why do you put up with that?" she asked her mom, after Rick left the house one day. "It's nothing, really," her mom assured her. "He's just worried about finding work. I'm sure it won't happen again." Shira doesn't share her mother's confidence.

Ben is in trouble again. His mother found a bag of white powder hidden behind the toilet: cocaine. Marcy isn't surprised. She thought that her brother might still be using drugs, even after getting busted and starting therapy. When he didn't show up at the family therapy meeting last week, Marcy suspected he was getting high but made an excuse for him. She said he had to make up a test he had missed. She thought that it would be best if she kept things calm in the family—a move that she regrets now.

Marcy was there when her mom confronted Ben about the cocaine. "Give it to me!" he yelled at their mother. When she wouldn't, he started swearing at her and then lunged for her, diving right over the coffee table and tipping it over. He slammed their mother into a wall, and she bumped her head but threw the bag into the aquarium. Ben shoved his mother again, really hard, and then pulled over the whole wall unit in a rage. The television, the stereo, and the aquarium crashed to the floor. By then Marcy's stomach was killing her—it always acted up when there was a scene with Ben. She knew she had to do something this time—Ben was out of control. She dialed 911 and reported her brother to the police.

Defining "Dysfunction"

As previously discussed, all families go through periods of stress, during which they don't function particularly well. And occasional conflict breaks out even in the healthiest of families. At these times, family members work together to resolve their differences and support one another until the stressful event passes. They usually manage to work things out.

Sometimes families don't function well on an ongoing basis. These families are said to be "dysfunctional." Just as any family can be healthy, regardless of its structure, any family can be dysfunctional. In general, a dysfunctional family is one that fails to meet some or all of the basic needs of its members. Sometimes these needs, such as food, shelter, or clothing, are so basic that people take them for granted. More often, emotional needs, such as the need for love, support, and security, go unmet.

Although a family can be dysfunctional in several different ways, there are some characteristics of dysfunction that occur more frequently than others. The following are common ways that dysfunction can show up in families. In many families, more than one of these circumstances is involved.

- **Mismanaged conflict.** This occurs when family members can't resolve conflict when it comes up and either end up fighting constantly or avoid the conflict completely so that it is never confronted and settled. Either way, when conflicts are not handled well, important issues can remain unresolved.
- **Mismanaged anger.** One family member may not know how to control his or her anger and takes it out on others in inappropriate ways, ranging from withdrawal of affection—the "silent treatment"—to verbal or physical abuse.
- **Alcohol, drugs, and other forms of dependence.** When one or more family member is dependent on alcohol or drugs, a host of issues can arise. These can include codependency, which happens when others in a family are controlled by a loved one's addiction.
- **Neglect and abuse.** Abuse occurs when one family member harms another physically, sexually, or emotionally.

It's important to remember that just because a family is dysfunctional does not mean that its members do not love one another. Instead, dysfunction usually results from a host of problems in the lives of parents and caregivers. Parents usually do the best they can with their children, but the truth is that they're human too and can't always manage the difficult task of parenting if they are over-whelmed by their own troubles. It could be that their parenting skills have been impaired by mental or physical illness or simply by ignorance. In addition, many parents of dysfunctional families grew up in unhealthy or abusive families themselves and don't know how to break the mold. It may be hard for a person growing up in a dysfunctional family to believe it, but the truth is that poor parenting is rarely intentional.

All that aside, it's also true that the impact of dysfunction on a family's children and teenagers can be very destructive. A healthy family provides a safe environment for teenagers to grow and deal with the many changes adolescence brings, offering the right balance between independence and guidance. Dysfunctional families can disturb that process in several ways. If the problem is one of structure—boundaries that are overly rigid, lax, or inconsistent—family life can be simply confusing. Young people in these families often don't know what is expected of them and what is an appropriate behavior or choice in any given situation. Let's say, for example, a parent never asks his or her children where they are going when they leave home at night and never gives them a time that they need to be back home. Those teenagers would have a harder time knowing what types of behavior or activities are appropriate than those whose parents have set rules for when their sons or daughters can and cannot go out.

If parents and caregivers are so impaired by illness or dependence on drugs or alcohol that they are unable to manage their homes, teenagers may be inappropriately forced to take on adult roles, such as caring full-time for a younger sibling. If children are neglected or abused, they may grow up thinking they are worthless and end up developing low self-esteem and feelings of shame and anger.

Finally, the family in which a person grows up serves as a model for that young person's future. If dysfunction is the only thing children know, they stand a chance of repeating that pattern when they start their own families later on. It is important to remember that all patterns can be broken. Although growing up in a dysfunctional home can be painful and even damaging, there are ways to replace unhealthy behavior with healthy behavior.

Coping with Mismanaged Conflict and Anger

Ben has been sent to a detention facility for three months. He takes classes and is getting drug and anger counseling. The only time Marcy sees him is at her family's weekly therapy sessions. He's pretty quiet, though, just answering "yes" or "no" when the therapist asks him a direct question. He seems pretty angry with Marcy for calling the police that day. He won't even look her in the eye.

Conflict and anger are a big topic during their sessions. Yesterday the therapist asked Marcy how she thought their family dealt with problems. "Badly," was Marcy's first response. But that got her thinking about how they each reacted when something went wrong. Her parents got angry, yelling at each other and pointing fingers of blame, Ben clammed up, and she always tried to make the fighting stop. Nothing ever seemed to get resolved.

In Marcy's family, conflict and anger were not dealt with effectively and now the whole family is paying the price. Their inability to deal with differences contributed to Marcy's parents splitting up, but it didn't put an end to their fighting. Ben blew up in a way that got him arrested, and Marcy tried to make peace at all costs. As individuals and as a family, they need to learn more constructive ways of dealing with both conflict and anger, since both inevitably arise in the course of any relationship.

The following are common ways that people mismanage conflict and anger.

1. They try to deny anger or keep it inside and avoid all conflict. This is also known as "stuffing" anger. Anger is a valid emotion, just like happiness and sadness. If people don't learn how to express their anger and keep it inside, they might develop health problems, such as stomachaches, tension headaches, or heart disease. That's what sometimes happens to Marcy, who can't stand the sound of raised voices. She tries to avoid fighting with her parents and with friends, even if it means that she is left feeling tense or sad inside. Afterward, she often gets a stomachache and finds herself gritting her teeth.

2. They engage in passive-aggressive behavior. They manipulate others in ways that are hurtful but not entirely obvious. If a mother thinks her daughter has gained weight, and she says something like "your sister's nice and thin these days, isn't she?" that's an example of a passive-aggressive statement. What the mother really means in this case is that she thinks her daughter needs to lose a few pounds, but she doesn't come out and say it. In some ways, it would be easier for the daughter if the mother were more straightforward, because then they could have an honest conversation about it. As it is, there is little the daughter can say to the mother, who could just deny that she meant anything accusing when she said what she did. And it could well be that the mother is not aware that she is being accusing. Sometimes the passive-aggressive individual may not realize that he or she is engaging in hurtful behavior, which makes it easy to deny anything. For an in-depth discussion of passive-aggressive behavior, see *Straight Talk About Anger,* by Christine Dentemaro and Rachel Kranz, another volume in this series.

3. They retreat into silence. Ben withdraws whenever he is angry and upset. This means that even though he may be unhappy with something that has happened in the family, he doesn't say that he is—he just stops talking

altogether. So it was always easy for Marcy to know when Ben was angry—even before he started doing drugs—but it was also always impossible for her to know why. She had to guess and try to make things better. Silence can be punishing when it is used as a way to express anger. It allows the person who is angry to control the situation, because someone else is left wondering what he or she did wrong. Silence used in this way does nothing to resolve the problem at hand.

4. They blow up. Some people who don't express their anger in a healthy manner may find themselves blowing up over minor things. Their reaction may be out of all proportion to what has happened. Anger that is denied expression usually finds another way to come out. Ben was upset when his mother confronted him about the cocaine, but his reaction was completely uncontrolled.

5. They become aggressive. Aggressive behavior is used to dominate, hurt, or control others. People who constantly initiate arguments and yell and scream until they get their way are using a form of aggression. Another type of aggression is physical violence. Anger that is expressed violently amounts to abuse.

With the exception of violent behavior, these expressions of anger become truly dysfunctional only when they are repeated patterns of behavior. Again, they rarely resolve issues effectively and just leave at least someone, and usually everyone, feeling frustrated and unfulfilled. And they can have long-lasting effects. If a parent or caregiver is totally uncomfortable with conflict and expressions of anger, he or she may avoid confrontations with children and teenagers entirely, which results in a failure to set limits—a failure to provide structure for young people. An aggressive parent or caregiver who may want to control everything a teenager does may not give that teen freedom to make any independent decisions, thus not allowing him or her to experience the consequences of those decisions. That may result in a young adult who lacks confidence and sense of responsibility. And again, later in life, children often model what they have seen growing up. If they have learned inappropriate expressions of anger early on, they are likely to repeat them.

How to Change?

If you or someone you are close with are having intense feelings of anger, there are ways that you can manage it. *In Straight Talk About Anger*, authors Christine Dentemaro and Rachel Kranz suggest that it first helps to acknowledge your angry feelings. Acknowledging them helps you to identify the source of your anger so that you can take steps to deal with it constructively. They have these suggestions for exploring and acknowledging your angry feelings.

- Write about them. Keep a journal or diary.
- Keep an "anger log." Every time you feel angry, jot down why. What's happening? What time of day is it? Who are you angry with? Eventually you may be able to spot a pattern and identify specific things or behaviors that make you angry.
- Talk to a friend. This can give you both a sense of relief and a deeper understanding of your feelings. Marcy always knows that she can unload on her best friend, Annie. Since Annie is a good listener, she helps Marcy clarify what she's really angry about.
- Pay attention to your dreams. Write them down. They often reveal deeply hidden thoughts and feelings.

Dentemaro and Kranz also suggest that in order to be in the best shape to deal constructively with your anger, you take care of yourself—eating well, getting enough sleep, and exercising to release tension.

If you are faced with someone else's anger, try to limit the extent to which they can take it out on you. That is called being "assertive." You are insisting on being treated well, which is always your right. You may not be able to control another person's behavior, but you can let them know how their behavior is affecting you. For example, you can tell someone who is speaking to you in an angry or aggressive way that it is making you uncomfortable. Tell that person that you will be glad to talk about the problem when he or she stops yelling and can discuss things calmly. If you realize that someone is manipulating you with passive-aggressive behavior, you might tell that person that he or she is hurting your feelings or simply ask him or her to stop.

Effective Communication and Conflict Resolution

In the end, coping with mismanaged conflict and anger is all about replacing unhealthy approaches with healthy ones. In chapter 2, you learned about the ways healthy families communicate and deal with conflict. The members of healthy families may argue with one another from time to time, but as a rule they don't take out their anger and frustrations on one another or pick fights with the sole intent of winning and getting their way. Instead, they try to work through an issue until it is resolved. Instead of blaming and attacking one another, they focus on the problem, exploring their different perspectives and truly listening to one another. They focus on their needs and feelings, not solely on the outcome they desire. They try to find solutions that really allow them all to win. When they can't resolve their differences, they might try another approach. If tempers are really running high, they might take a cooling-off period.

If you are seeking a way to communicate with the members of your family in a healthier way, it may be a good idea to use the principles of effective communication discussed in chapter 2. They are:

1. Approach other family members with respect. Avoid criticism, negativity, and ridicule.
2. Use "I" messages.
3. Practice active listening. Pay attention, don't interrupt, observe body language, and clarify.

Of course, trying to replace an entire family's unhealthy behaviors with healthy ones is not something one person—particularly a teenager—should be expected to do on his or her own. The behaviors listed above are meant to give you guidance on your own communication with your family, but you will probably need help in trying to convince your family to adopt them as well. There are family therapists who specialize in helping families communicate with one another in healthier ways, and other places to go for help and support. For more on this, see the "Getting Help" section in chapter 6.

Coping with Dependence

Dependence means that a person uses alcohol or drugs regularly and habitually, to the extent that he or she can't do without them. If a person craves alcohol or a psychoactive drug and feels distressed without it, that person has what is called a "psychological dependence." "Physical dependence," or addiction, occurs when a person's body becomes so used to the presence of drugs or alcohol that it will go through withdrawal symptoms (such as nausea, vomiting, and sleeplessness) without it. A person dependent in any way on alcohol or drugs is practicing substance abuse.

A person who is dependent on alcohol or drugs can make life unpredictable, unpleasant, and even dangerous for other family members. The problem is especially severe when the dependence is that of a parent or caregiver. One who is drunk, high, coming off a high, or hung over is prone to extreme and sudden mood swings. As Shira knows, Rick can be passive or mean, even violent, when he is drunk. When he is sober, on the other hand, he can be kind and even loving at times. She never knows what to expect when she sees him.

That sort of unpredictability can mean that substance abusing caregivers are not always there physically or emotionally for other family members. They may forget important appointments and promises. They may be inconsistent in providing structure and setting healthy limits for their children. Their general irresponsibility may force teenagers to take on family responsibilities such as making sure bills are paid, meals are made, or other children are cared for properly. Like Shira, teenagers in these families may face embarrassment or have to "cover" and lie for the problem drinker or drug user. In many cases, they may overlook their own needs, feelings, and desires. Overall, substance abusers are poor role models, failing to demonstrate healthy choices relating to drinking, drug use, handling stress, and other forms of risky behavior.

Substance abusers put their families at risk in other ways. They often face financial problems, using family funds to support their habits. They may have trouble finding and keeping jobs. And many will become involved in illegal activities ranging from driving while intoxicated to engaging in violent crimes to support a drug habit.

Finally, substance abuse is associated with physical and emotional abuse and damaging neglect of children and other family members. Alcohol and drugs interfere with a person's judgment and his or her inhibitions, both of which will increase the likelihood that they will act aggressively. According to a fact sheet published by the National Clearinghouse on Child Abuse and Neglect Information, which compiles data from various federal agencies, a 1993 study by the U.S. Department of Health and Human Services found that children from alcohol-abusing families were nearly 4 times more likely to be maltreated overall, almost

5 times more likely to be physically neglected, and 10 times more likely to be the victims of emotional neglect than children in families that weren't affected by alcohol abuse. The fact sheet refers to other studies that suggest 50 percent to 80 percent of all substantiated child abuse cases involve some degree of substance abuse by the child's caregivers. Substance abuse is also a factor in a majority of child neglect cases; in fact, neglect is the most common reason that child-welfare authorities remove children from the parents' custody. It also is involved in a large number of elder abuse and domestic violence cases. According to a 1993 study published in *Alcohol Health and Research World,* alcohol is involved in more than 50 percent of all incidents of domestic violence. You will learn more about violence and other types of abuse in families later in this chapter.

Breaking the Cycle: Understanding Codependency

Shira and her mother are cleaning out the attic. While sorting through some old photo albums, Shira finds a picture of her grandmother. She died before Shira was born. "How come you never talk about grandma?" she asks her mother. Her mom shrugs. "I guess we weren't that close. She was drunk a lot of the time and could be pretty difficult." "Isn't that interesting," Shira thinks to herself. "That's exactly the way I feel about Rick."

Shira has just found out something important about her mother and about the way alcohol and drug use affects families. People who grow up with substance abusers often form adult relationships with other substance abusers. As a result, they continue their exposure to and involvement in the dysfunctional behavior that they knew as children. They remain the caretakers for alcoholics and other addicts, often harming themselves and making it possible for the substance abuser to keep on abusing. That is called "enabling." That is what Shira's mother does when she makes excuses for Rick's drinking or when she buys alcohol for him. The overall pattern of this kind of behavior is commonly called "codependency."

Codependency can show up in other ways, at home, at work, and in relationships outside the family. A codependent adult may

- generally have trouble forming and maintaining healthy relationships;
- confuse pity for another person (the substance abuser) with love;
- constantly put the needs of others before his or her own;
- find it hard to trust others;
- try to constantly please others;
- feel an extreme need to control others;
- be a perfectionist and never be satisfied with his or her own achievements;
- have a low sense of self-worth; and/or
- feel sad, angry, scared, or lonely much of the time.

All of these are unhealthy forms of behavior, harmful to the codependent adult's well-being. That harm can be physical, as well as emotional, if codependency keeps him or her trapped in a relationship with a substance abuser who is also abusive. Codependent adults need to first recognize their symptoms and then seek help in breaking old patterns of behavior. For a teenager growing up with an alcoholic or drug user, learning about these long-term problems underscores the need to act immediately to break these cycles.

Getting Help

Shira realizes that she needs help coping not only with Rick's dependence but with her mother's codependency. She remembers seeing a commercial on television about a place called Al-Anon that offers assistance to people who have been affected by a family member's drinking. One day when she has some extra time at the computer lab in school, she logs on to the Internet. Shira discovers that Al-Anon has a specific division for teenagers, called Alateen. She also finds out that most cities and towns throughout the country have a local Alateen chapter. (For more information on how to contact Al-Anon or Alateen, see chapter 6.)

On Al-Anon's web site Shira goes through its checklist that helps family members confirm whether they are being affected by another's problem drinking. It confirms for her that she has been affected by Rick's drinking. Among others, she can easily answer "yes" to the questions asking if she ever worried about how much someone drinks and whether she had ever been hurt or embarrassed by a drinker's behavior. Shira takes down the address of the local Alateen chapter. She thinks she might need it some day.

If you, like Shira, are dealing with a family member's dependence on drugs or alcohol, there are some steps you can take to help deal with it, even if the drinker or drug user is unwilling to admit that he or she has a problem.

1. Contact a self-help organization like Alateen or Nar-A-Teen. If you attend a local meeting, you will be able to meet other teenagers in similar situations and share coping strategies. All information disclosed at meetings is strictly confidential.

2. Try to understand that you cannot control another person's behavior and are not responsible in any way for their drinking or drug use. You can only control the way you react—whether you worry about that person's problem, whether you continue to cover up for him or her, thereby helping the drinker or drug user continue with the dependency. This is a fundamental belief of these self-help organizations.

3. Make contact with supportive adults outside your home. You can talk to a friend's parent, a teacher, coach, or school counselor about the situation at home. Even if you are not comfortable talking to that person about the drinking or drug use in your family, this type of

relationship could give you a way to receive the healthy advice, direction, and even affection that you may not be finding at home.

4. Seek help in restoring your own damaged feelings of self-esteem and self-worth. In chapter 6, you will learn where to go to find groups that can help you, as well as sources that can put you in touch with professional help.

Recovery

It is comforting to think that when a family member seeks help for his or her addiction that everything will get better. Certainly that's always a step in the right direction. But alcoholism and drug dependence are illnesses. Recovery takes time. It is a process that can be hard on families.

Recent research conducted by the Family Recovery Project at the Mental Research Institute in Palo Alto, California, focused on the ways families handled recovery from alcoholism. The researchers found that the early stages of recovery, which can last as long as three to five years, can be disruptive and even traumatic to the family as a whole. That's largely because recovering drinkers often have to become totally self-absorbed in order to get over their addiction. They may end up emotionally neglecting their children as a result. The researchers emphasized the importance of children having outside support—trusted adults, counselors, peers, and support groups—through this period. They also offered hope for families. While recovery is a life-long process for an alcoholic or drug addict, people who are trying to overcome addiction can eventually establish a safe and stable family life.

Recovery can also be hard on the whole family when the substance abuser is a teenager. While most families focus on getting a teenager to stop using drugs, this is only the first step in the process. According to a 1995 Brown University study, while the teenager was using the drugs the family may have been reacting only to the issue of substance abuse and the difficult behavior it provoked. When the teenager stops using the drugs, the focus of the family must change in order to help him or her stay clean. This means that family members may have to acknowledge how they may have enabled the teen's drug use. Parents and caregivers may have to learn better methods for setting limits and providing structure for the teenagers. The whole process can raise feelings within the family that can be hard for everybody involved—and when things get tough, substance-abusing teens are at the greatest risk of relapse. The entire family may need a support system, including school officials, counselors, and therapists, to help them through this long and difficult process.

Coping with Abuse and Neglect

Things between Rick and Shira's mother are getting worse. Not only has he hit her—her eye is all purple and swollen—but when he's drunk he's cruel and aggressive. "You're dragging me down, Carol," he snarled last night after a few drinks. "If you weren't so stupid and so scared of any kind of change, we could have moved on from this dead-end town a long time ago. We could've really made a go of things. It's all your damned fault."

Rick's behavior toward Shira's mother has become abusive. Abuse is the maltreatment of one family member by another. The abuser can be a parent or caregiver, a sibling, a child, or any other member of the household or extended family. Abuse usually follows some sort of established and progressive pattern, meaning that it usually gets worse with time if nothing is done to end it.

Abuse can come from any member of a family, including parents, siblings, and spouses. The following are the most common types of abuse that are directed at children and teenagers in families.

- **Physical.** This is any type of physical violence directed at one family member by another. It can take the form of hitting, scratching, burning, punching—anything that causes physical harm.
- **Emotional.** This can include constant unjustified criticism, belittling, and put-downs directed at one family member or another. It can also take the form of persistent and cruel teasing and taunting or one family member frightening another. Emotional abuse can also involve the withholding of love and affection. (See "Neglect," below.)
- **Sexual.** *Incest* is traditionally defined as sexual relations between blood relatives. Many people now adopt a broader definition, including sexual relations between a child and anyone who is in a position of authority over and trust with that child. The National Committee to Prevent Child Abuse defines child sexual abuse as "forced, tricked, or coerced sexual behavior between a young person and an older person." It may include any of the following acts: nudity, disrobing, genital exposure, observation of the child, kissing, fondling, masturbation, oral-genital contact, child pornography, penetration with fingers, and vaginal or anal intercourse. More than one-third of female victims of child sexual abuse are abused by relatives. About one-tenth of boys who are abused are abused by relatives.
- **Neglect.** Neglect can be physical, which occurs when essential health or medical services are withheld or a child's physical needs for food, clothing, and shelter are not met. When love and affection are withheld, the neglect is said to be emotional. Emotional neglect, like physical neglect, can block a child's psychological growth and development.

Other forms of abuse that occur within families include the abuse of one domestic partner by another and elder abuse.

Partner abuse is also known as "spouse abuse" or "domestic violence." It includes any mistreatment of one domestic partner by the other. They can be married, living together, or just dating, gay or straight. The abuse can take the form of physical or emotional abuse, threats of violence, or sexual mistreatment. Nonconsensual sex between domestic partners amounts to rape. Another form of abuse between domestic partners, closely tied to emotional abuse, is financial: One partner takes the other's money and often refuses to release it even for necessities. This amounts to a form of control by one over the other. While the U.S. Justice Department estimates that 95 percent of partner abuse is directed at women by men, men can also be victims. In some cases, abuse between partners is mutual.

Elder abuse is the physical, emotional, sexual, or financial abuse of elderly family members. Aged and infirm family members can also be the victims of neglect, if they are dependent on others to provide for their physical and medical care.

What Motivates Abuse and Neglect?

Abuse is never justified; the victim is never at fault. Instead, it is always indicative of a problem in the abuser's life. Abusers are deeply insecure individuals who may seek to make up for their insecurities by controlling others. They may have been abused as children and are repeating a cycle of violence and hurt that they learned early on. In short, abuse is about misdirected anger and frustration. There are always better ways to resolve conflicts and release anger.

Alcohol and drugs are often involved in abusive family situations. In her book *To Be an Anchor in the Storm: A Guide for Families and Friends of Abused Women*, Susan Brewster states that these are closely connected but separate problems. Alcohol or drug use may make the abuse more severe than it might otherwise be, but they probably don't cause an otherwise nonviolent person to become violent. Even without the substance abuse, the abuser would likely be emotionally abusive at least. Both problems—the dependency and the abuse—need to be treated if the abuse is to end.

In spite of abusers' apologies and claims to the contrary, abuse can rarely be considered unintentional. The only time it might be is if the abuse was triggered by extreme mental illness. Neglect, on the other hand, sometimes is unintended. In some cases, a caregiver may be so impaired by illness or so lacking in parenting skills that he or she cannot attend to the needs of children and other family members. The caregiver may not even be aware of what basic caregiving entails. Infants and very young children are at the greatest risk of being harmed through extreme physical and emotional neglect.

How Are Children and Teenagers Affected by Abuse?

Abuse is destructive to every individual involved and to the collective family health. It is particularly so to children and teenagers in the home, whether they are the direct victims of abuse or witnesses to abuse at home.

For children who are victims of abuse, it is the ultimate betrayal of trust by a family member. They are likely to feel shame and misplaced guilt for somehow bringing the abuse on themselves. If children and teenagers are told with words and violent acts that they are worthless, they'll feel worthless. Their inability to protect themselves from harm shatters their self-esteem further. Other common emotional problems are withdrawal, an inability to trust others, isolation, anxiety, depression, and anger. Finally, abuse sends a message to its young victims that violent, intimidating, and abusive behavior is acceptable in intimate relationships.

That lesson is also passed on to young people who witness domestic abuse in their homes. Like children who are abused directly, witnesses risk becoming abusers or victims in future relationships. They are profoundly affected in other ways as well. Their inability to stop the abuse can leave them feeling powerless, with a feeling of failure and low self-worth. If they are ashamed of the situation at home and concerned about keeping it secret—a situation that is often encouraged by the adult victim—they may withdraw from friends and nonfamily members, becoming socially isolated. They may find themselves consumed with worry for the safety of their abused parents, caregivers, or siblings, just as Shira is starting to feel about her mother.

Young people who grow up in abusive homes are also affected by its physical and emotional toll on the caregiver who is being abused. They are harmed indirectly because an abused parent or caregiver is likely to be distracted, irritable, and inconsistent. She or he probably can't even truly help children deal with their fears about the situation. If abusers are teaching children to act aggressively, their victims may be avoiding confrontations with their children entirely. This can be unhealthy in its own right, leading to such problems as a failure to set and enforce limits.

What Are the Effects of Neglect?

Children and teenagers are neglected physically when their basic needs for food, shelter, or clothing aren't met or their medical conditions are left untreated. They can be neglected emotionally in any number of ways. They may be left alone for long periods of time; they can be treated with cold indifference, never told that they are loved; or their achievements can go without praise and unnoticed. To develop a sense of self-worth, everyone needs to be told and shown that they are worthy of affection and treated with respect.

Recent research indicates that children need affectionate care from their earliest days. Scientists in the United
States are getting a unique—and unfortunate—opportunity to study the long-term effects of neglect as they treat
the problems of certain children who were adopted in
the past decade from overseas orphanages, particularly
from orphanages in eastern European countries. While
these children were fed, they often didn't have the
opportunity to bond with dedicated and affectionate
caregivers. In some cases, infants in understaffed orphanages were left in cribs for long periods of time—18
to 20 hours per day—with just a feeding bottle. They
were not cuddled, talked to, or played with. Later, when
they were adopted into loving families in North America,
many displayed a range of problems including motor
difficulties, hyperactivity, learning disabilities, and severe emotional and behavioral problems. Some were
unable to bond with their new adoptive families, appar-
ently suffering from a condition commonly referred to
as "attachment disorder."

According to child development experts Linda Mayes
and Sally Provence, as quoted in a May 1998 article in
the *New York Times Magazine*, children need continuous
affectionate care by one or a small number of caregivers
in order to develop emotionally. They need to learn that
someone will comfort them when they are upset in order
to learn how to later comfort themselves and later still,
to give comfort to others. In other words, people learn
how to love, to be caring and affectionate through early
reliance on others. And the damage gross neglect can
cause is not just emotional. A lack of stimulation and
emotional contact in the first three years, in particular,
can actually harm brain development, as it relates to the
ability to receive and express emotions.

It is important to note that many of these children who
have experienced severe neglect have responded both
to treatment and to the affection they have found in their

adoptive homes. Some may experience long-term problems, but their situation underscores the life-long importance of early care and affectionate bonding, and the hazards of neglect.

Stopping Abuse and Neglect

If you have been abused or feel that you are being neglected, it is critical to your own well-being that it be stopped. Here are some things you can do.

1. Tell someone. This is a crucial first step. Talk to a trusted adult about what has happened to you. This could be a parent or caregiver, a friend's parent, a teacher, a family doctor, a coach, or a school adviser. In some dysfunctional homes it isn't uncommon for other family members to deny the possibility that there is an abuser in their midst. If the first person you tell refuses to listen, tell someone else. Don't be discouraged. Confiding in a friend may help you get the courage to reach out to someone who can truly help you.

2. Call a hot line or the police. Agencies offering professional help to abused children and teenagers exist across the country, and most run hot lines. You can generally find these numbers on the first page of the phone book and in the Yellow Pages. (For national hot line numbers, see Chapter Six.) You can call a hot line in addition to or in place of talking to a trusted adult. The person you speak to will be trained to give you advice as to how to stop the abuse and where to go.

3. If possible, refuse all unwanted advances. If you are uncomfortable with someone's touch, or even with their talk, tell them. You can say "Stop," or "I want you to leave now." However, if you do not speak up or stop

the abuse, do not blame yourself. It is extremely difficult to react when you are scared or feel under a threat of violence or other abuse. Failing to stop the abuser does not imply consent on your part.

4. If you are uncomfortable being left alone with another person, your mother's boyfriend or a brother or sister, for example, say so. Even if what you fear is another person's relentless teasing, you should try not to expose yourself to it. But again, if you are exposed to it in spite of what you have said, do not blame yourself. Keep in mind that abuse of any type is never the fault of the victim.

5. Try to form relationships with adults outside your family who will provide you with the positive care, influence, and support that you need.

Many teenagers in abusive situations wonder what will happen to them and to their families if they disclose the abuse. They sometimes fear that they will be taken away from their homes and placed with strangers, losing friends and school connections in the process. They feel guilty about breaking up their family. And they may fear that their family situation will be publicized.

It usually doesn't happen that way. If the police or other authorities become involved, the abuser probably will have to leave the home until the situation is investigated and the abuser gets much needed treatment. Generally the victim and the family as a whole are also given help in the form of counseling. The young victim of abuse is unlikely to be taken out of the home and placed in foster care unless he or she is at any risk of further abuse; the victim would still be in some danger, for example, if the nonabusing parent refuses to sever contact with an abusing partner, or is also an abuser. In neglect cases, children are sometimes taken away from their parents and caregivers until a safe environment can be provided.

If the abuse or neglect results in criminal charges and a trial, the identity of the underage victim will not be disclosed publicly. If disclosing the name of the abuser results in disclosing the name of the victim, the abuser's name will not be published.

These are tough issues for any teenager to face. But if you are being abused, try not to let them deter you from taking steps to end it. It isn't fair to yourself to risk additional harm and a safe future for fear of upsetting other members of your family.

Stopping the Abuse or Neglect of a Loved One

Shira is starting to see big changes in her mom. She used to be a lot of fun; now she's jumpy and distracted much of the time. She talks in a whisper if Rick is around, even if he's watching TV in another room. She never goes out by herself anymore, because Rick doesn't like it when she does. When Shira thinks about it, her mom hasn't made any friends since she started seeing Rick. She's also lost touch with her own family, such as her sisters and her father. Rick always insisted they never liked him.

The situation at home has Shira really worried. If Rick gets more violent, what will happen to her mother after Shira moves out? Shira is starting to think that her mom should just leave Rick and get her own fresh start. But her mother isn't even ready to admit that she is being treated badly!

To Shira, it seems obvious that her mother is being mistreated. But if she could see the situation from her mother's perspective, things would look less clear. When he isn't drinking, Rick can be the sweet, charming guy she first fell for. He tells her that he loves her, so much so that he's jealous when another man even looks at her. He has promised that he'll never hit her again. He's just going through a bad time, as she's told Shira.

If you want to help a loved one deal with partner abuse, it helps to understand the complex mind-set of the victim.

Like Shira's mom, victims of partner abuse often minimize it, if they talk about it at all. They do so for many reasons, according to social worker Susan Brewster (author of *To Be an Anchor in the Storm: A Guide for Families and Friends of Abused Women*). They might feel embarrassed or ashamed, responsible for the abuse in some way, fearful of what their partners may do if they talk about the abuse or threaten to leave, concerned about burdening others (like their teenage children) with their problems, or even protective of their abusive partners, whom they often truly love. Like Shira's mother, many abuse victims have so much invested emotionally in their partners that they refuse to admit that they are capable of harm. They have often been emotionally and physically isolated from supportive friends and family—at the instigation of the abuser, who generally wants to control all aspects of his or her partner's life. Their self-esteem and confidence have been worn away.

The decision to leave or change an abusive relationship can only be that of the victim. You can't "rescue" a loved one in that situation. Since domestic violence is about control, the abused partner has to make a change by actively taking control back from the abuser, not handing it over to a third party. Even so, there are things that you can do to help. Here are some possible approaches (adapted from Susan Brewster and from Dawn Bradley Berry's *The Domestic Violence Sourcebook*).

1. If she or he chooses to talk to you, listen actively and without passing judgment. The abuser is already making the victim feel "weak" for submitting to the abuse. Don't suggest that you also feel that he or she is weak for staying in the relationship.
2. Offer to talk and to help whenever he or she needs you.
3. If you ask directly about the source of injuries or whether your loved one is being abused in some way, don't challenge his or her denial. Again, just offer your help any time.

4. If you don't live together, for example if the victim is a sister who lives with an abusive partner, keep in touch even if she doesn't initiate contact. You don't always have to be talking about or dwelling on the abuse. Just calling and talking about everyday things helps to build a sense of trust and a feeling that someone cares. It helps to lessen the sense of isolation that many victims of abuse feel.

5. Try to read between the lines. If you feel your loved one may be approaching the subject indirectly, for instance by saying "Bob has been kind of upset lately," ask for some clarification. "What do you mean by that?"

6. Don't urge your loved one to leave the abusive partner before he or she is ready.

7. Once the abuse is out in the open, reassure the victim that he or she is not to blame or deserving of it in any way. It helps to remind victims of their special skills and abilities, since their feelings of self-worth and competence may be badly eroded.

8. Do some research. Find out what agencies and organizations exist to help people who want to get out of abusive situations. Make a list of contacts and phone numbers that you can give to your loved one at the appropriate time. In this context, ask yourself if there is something special to consider about this relationship and if special help may be needed. A woman who is new to this country, for example, may be fearful of deportation if she seeks to escape her relationship, but the 1994 Federal Violence Against Women Act protects them in these situations. Homosexuals may fear that seeking help to end an abusive relationship will force him or her to "come out" publicly, but many organizations now offer special services for abused gays and lesbians. Doing some homework doesn't mean becoming an expert on the law. The people staffing a hot line or shelter will be able to direct your loved one to the proper assistance.

Helping someone in an abusive relationship can be frustrating and takes a tremendous amount of courage and emotional maturity. The abusive relationship is often so complex and the victim so emotionally tied to the abuser that battered women, in particular, usually return to their partners several times before leaving for good. Some even blame the people who helped them for pushing them away from their relationship or even accuse them of making up the abuse. If you want to help a loved one confront an abusive situation, you may want to confide in a trusted adult and let them support and guide you through the process. And should your abused loved one choose to stay with his or her abusive partner in the end, remember that you are not at fault in any way.

If you suspect that a child or an elderly person is being abused in some way, you should immediately confide your fears to a trusted adult. He or she will take the necessary steps to notify the authorities.

Healing the Wounds and Breaking the Cycle

Stopping abuse and neglect is a necessary first step toward a healthy, happy, and safe future. Whether you were the victim of neglect or abuse or witnessed it in your home, you have to take steps to heal the pain it has caused. You may have lingering feelings of anger toward your abuser or other members of your family. If you are separated from your family or if the abuser has left the home, you may be experiencing feelings of loss. You will need to repair the damage to your own feelings of safety and self-worth that neglect, abuse, or exposure to abuse has caused.

It is hard to do this alone. Counseling can help. A peer support group can help you deal with feelings of shame and isolation that are common among abused and neglected teens. You can find out what help is available through your school counselor or through the hot lines that are listed at the front of your telephone book. National hot line numbers are also listed in chapter 6.

As you know by now, many abusers and adult victims of abuse are repeating behavior that they experienced as children. If you were abused or exposed to it at home, it helps to take steps to avoid having the cycle repeat later in your life. These include learning how to handle conflict and anger constructively and nonviolently and to set limits on the type of behavior you will tolerate (see "Coping with Mismanaged Conflict and Anger," earlier in this chapter).

In order to avoid becoming a victim of domestic violence in later life, you should be sensitive to behavior that may indicate that the person you are involved with is potentially dangerous. Your partner might become abusive if he or she

- is extremely jealous, even of friends and family;
- grew up in a violent home;
- sometimes uses force or violence to solve problems;
- has a quick temper, which can be set off by small frustrations;
- throws or breaks things when angry;
- demonstrates cruelty to animals;
- has very rigid expectations of gender roles, for instance thinking women should always submit to the needs and desires of men;
- repeatedly tries to tell you what to do and where to go and tries to keep tabs on you;
- humiliates you verbally;
- puts down and actively discourages your personal plans and goals, such as going to college or traveling;
- tries to manipulate you with guilt;
- intimidates you with threatening looks or actions or with weapons that he or she threatens to use against you;

- uses coercion and threats to keep you in the relationship, for instance threatening to hurt you or commit suicide if you break up;
- controls your money; and/or
- treats you roughly and physically forces you to do things you would not otherwise do.

If your partner does some of these things, he or she may already be emotionally abusive. It may be worth your while to consider whether you really want to remain in the relationship.

Moving On

The proof that dysfunctional behavior can be changed and replaced by healthy behavior can be found in the statistics of abuse victims who later become abusers. The figures vary, but it is clear that many people who were abused in some way as children *do not* repeat the cycle, as abusers or as victims.

As many teenagers know who are growing up in dysfunctional or abusive homes, you can't control the way other people behave toward you. But you can take control of your own future, by changing the way you react, by changing your own behavior and attitudes, and by taking measures to protect yourself and your family from dysfunction later on in life. In this way, you are breaking the cycle of dependence and beginning a new life, one that is as healthy as you want to make it.

5

Looking Ahead

Ira feels pretty settled at his new school. Taking his father's advice, he joined the drama club and through it has met people with similar interests. He's even been seeing someone for a couple of months. Her name is Shelley, and she's really into African-American drama and dance. She dragged Ira to an African dance workshop with her last week. He was a bit self-conscious, but the workshop was fun.

Shelley gets along well with Ira's family, but she's also curious about Ira's birth family and is pushing Ira to find out more. "I mean, you aren't ever going to be white like them," she said to him yesterday. "You owe it to yourself to explore your black side. Find out where you *really* come from."

Ira tells Shelley that he feels his adoptive family has made him the person he is. Still, he does admit to being increasingly curious about his birth family. But when he's talked about it with his parents, they've advised him to wait until he is an adult to search. It just seems like a long way off.

Even though she's going to a local college next year, Shira has decided to move into the dorms instead of remaining at home. She just can't stand being around Rick.

He's drinking more than ever, and his temper is getting worse. She worries that after she leaves Rick will become more abusive toward her mother but doesn't think staying is a solution either. I'll be there if and when mom really needs me, she tells herself. I just have to get on with my own life.

Because she wants to understand more about alcoholism, Shira decides to check out an Alateen meeting at a local church. At the meeting, she hears other young people talk about the way a family member's drinking has affected their home lives. One girl said that she came from three generations of problem drinkers. Shira is more determined than ever that if there is any family pattern of getting involved with drinkers, she's going to be the one to break it.

Eli has a new part-time job. He's working in an auto parts store that specializes in hard-to-find parts for old cars. The owner, Mr. Tyler, was a friend of his grandfather's. He approached Eli, because, he said, "You have to know cars. You learned from the best." Eli's mother encouraged him to take the job, hoping it might help him cope better with his grandfather's death.

Eli likes the job. It's good to be working on cars. And he really likes his boss. Mr. Tyler reminds him a lot of his grandfather. He has Bud's relaxed way of dealing with people, which puts his employees and customers alike at ease. And he seems to genuinely care about the people—students, mostly—who work for him. He always asks how their classes are going, trying to make sure that their after-school jobs aren't getting in the way of their school work.

Annie's mother's partner, Lin, has been living with them for a year now. Annie feels very comfortable with her. She wouldn't call Lin a stepmother exactly, but she's definitely part of the family. Annie cares about her.

In some ways, Annie thinks that having a lesbian mother has changed her. She probably has grown more tolerant of people's differences. But she's still careful about who she tells about her mom, confiding only in close friends, such as Marcy. It's hard to predict how others will react, although she doesn't worry as much about their reaction anymore.

Annie also finds herself worrying less about whether her father will get serious with the woman he's seeing. He's always been there for Annie and Lisa since the divorce. And seeing how happy her mother is in her new relationship, Annie thinks her dad deserves to have someone special in his life too.

Things are still tense in Marcy's family. Ben will be getting out of detention next week, and Marcy worries that he's still mad at her for getting him arrested in the first place. He doesn't talk much at all in their therapy sessions. Still, Marcy thinks that the counseling has helped. She's learning to express her own feelings better, even anger. Marcy's mother is seeing a therapist on her own, too, and seems to be dealing a bit better with issues surrounding the divorce. She doesn't spend the whole day in her bedroom anymore and has been talking about taking some computer classes at the community college. It's a first step, but Marcy knows they all have a long way to go toward working out their problems.

Marcy has found a real escape from family problems in photography. She's always enjoyed taking pictures, but she is now learning how to develop her own prints and has been exploring new techniques. She spends a lot of time in the photo lab at school. Annie even talked Marcy into entering a couple of pictures in a contest sponsored by the local newspaper, and to Marcy's surprise, she won second prize. That made her feel pretty good.

Taking Stock

At the end of childhood and adolescence lies young adulthood—and independence. You will probably leave your family home at some point, but that doesn't necessarily mean you will be breaking family bonds. You will remain a son or daughter, stepchild or grandchild, brother or sister, cousin, niece or nephew. You'll establish new relationships. At some point, you may choose to become a partner or parent. As an adult, it will be up to you to choose the kind of family ties you form and maintain, as well as the quality of those relationships.

What is for certain is that your family will in one way or another influence the choices you make. As you have learned, the family, regardless of its structure, is one of the strongest influences in a young person's life. Your family has taught you basic lessons about love, trust, sharing, and getting along with others. It has shaped the way you see yourself. It has provided you with a model of how a family functions.

That doesn't mean that you need to repeat and retain all aspects of your current family situation in your future relationships. You can keep those that you value, modify others, and leave some behind.

Take some time now to think about your family. Even if you feel angry or frustrated with various family members at the moment, stop and consider the things you have appreciated about them over the years. Maybe your father, stepmother, or grandparent has a special way of making you feel good about yourself, even when you are down. Your family may have certain rituals that are meaningful to you, for holidays and family celebrations, say. Maybe you and your sister or brother stay up all night talking and sharing secrets that you wouldn't share with anyone else.

Think, too, about some of the hard times your family has gone through. How were they handled by family members individually and as a group? Do you feel that the issues were effectively resolved?

Now think for a moment about areas in which your family may have fallen a bit short. Perhaps you wish that your family members didn't bicker as much or even that you all shared a meal together more often. You may have missed being more closely connected to aunts, uncles, and cousins.

You don't need to go looking for problems and flaws, but it helps to be aware of these things, positive and negative. In that way, you will start to become aware of qualities that are important to you when and if you start your own family.

Through the trials, errors, and good aspects of their respective family lives, the teenagers in this book all have some idea of the things that are important to them in family relationships. Shira, Annie, and Ira can all clearly acknowledge the value they place on respect in their family relationships. Shira knows that she would never become involved with a drinker—or if she inadvertently did, that she would end the relationship immediately. Annie admires the way her parents have treated each other, as well as her and Lisa, during the divorce and would like to think that she will always treat family members with kindness and compassion. Ira values how his parents have treated each of their three children fairly, and Eli knows his mother has done a fantastic job of raising him on her own. Still, he feels that a committed relationship between two adults is important if children are involved. Marcy thinks that good communication is crucial among family members and that even if the messages being communicated are negative ones, it is better that they are said and resolved than acted on in other, more damaging ways.

"Respect," "fairness," "sobriety," "communication," "commitment": Each of these young people will look and strive for the qualities he or she has identified, among others, in their continuing family relationships. They will do the same as they move into new roles in the future, potentially as partners and parents. That's because for each of these teens, these qualities amount to "values."

Clarifying Your Values

Values are the beliefs and ideals that matter most to an individual. They are the qualities and characteristics that set the standard for a person's own behavior and the behavior that he or she will look for in others. Examples of values that most people hold in common are honesty, loyalty, and compassion.

People reach an understanding of their values based on personal experience, and they may change somewhat over time. Annie, for instance, has come to realize how much she values acceptance. She never thought about it much before she found out that her mother was a lesbian, but now she feels strongly that people should be accepted for who they are, not singled out or condemned for their differences.

Take some time now to think about and list your own values. It may help to make a list of people you respect and try to pinpoint what it is about their behavior that you admire.

Having a strong sense of your values will help you set family and other life goals and help you make responsible decisions that you can live with. Staying true to your values will also give you the courage to stand by your choices, even if they come under criticism or attack from others simply for being "different" or untraditional in some way.

Setting Goals

Keeping in mind the principles of conduct that matter most to you—your values—think about your goals. It's early to make hard and fast decisions on your goals while you're still a teenager, and goals, like values, can change over time. Even so, setting goals and writing them down could help you sort out what kind of person you want to be and what types of career and relationships you want to have. For example, do you hope someday to establish a committed romantic partnership with another person? If so, do you think marriage may be a goal for you? Do you someday want to have children or, at this point, are you absolutely against the idea? As an adult, what sort of relationships do you hope to establish with your siblings, parents, or caregivers—those who have known you all your life?

Make a list of your goals. You may wish to group them under such headings as "education," "career," "family," "other." You may have separate lists of short-term and long-term goals. Under each goal, list some of the steps you think are required to get there. If you want to become a doctor, for example, you would need to go to college, satisfy pre-med requirements, complete medical school, an internship period, and possibly a residency that trains you in a specialty. The whole process will take 7 to 10 years, on average, and a considerable amount of money.

If you someday hope to be a parent, you may first aim to achieve a certain level of financial security. This will be particularly important if you feel strongly about staying home to raise your children. In this regard, you may feel the need to finish your education and achieve certain professional and financial goals before you start a family. Think of some things that might prevent you from reaching your goals.

Making a Responsible Decision

Starting to articulate personal and family values and goals will help you with some of the decisions that lie ahead. There will be a lot of them as you move from adolescence into young adulthood and toward independence. At various times, you may be faced with some of the following questions.

- Should you move out of your family home?
- Are you ready for a serious romantic relationship?
- Are you ready to be sexually active?
- Are you ready to live on your own? Or with someone else?
- Should you leave a relationship?
- Should you get married?
- Should you have children?

• Are you ready to be a parent?

If you keep your values and goals firmly in mind as you address these important questions, you are likely to be happier with the results. If Eli feels strongly that any children he has should have two parents, for instance, he is likely to think carefully about engaging in casual, unprotected sex, with its risk of pregnancy. He'll also think carefully about his readiness to make a commitment to another person. Shira will probably avoid starting a relationship with a man if she knows he has a history of physically abusing others. Most people feel bad about themselves or have nagging doubts if they make decisions that fly in the face of their core beliefs.

For many people, the best way to make important choices is to go through the following five-step process that can help them make a responsible decision.

1. State the question that needs to be resolved.
2. List the options.
3. Think through the positive and negative consequences of each option.
4. Weigh your options in light of your values and goals.
5. Make a decision.

Ira, for example, is considering the question of whether to search for his birth parents, and if so, whether he wants to do it now or later, when he's older. Here's how he is deciding these issues, using the five-step decision-making process.

1. State the question that needs to be resolved. Ira is thinking about these questions:
   • Should he undertake a search for his birth parents?
   • If so, when?
2. List the options. Ira has made the following list of his options:

- don't search
- collect information but don't act on it by contacting the birth parents
- collect information and make contact
- do it now, against his parents' advice
- wait five years before taking any steps

(If you are too close to a situation, you may not be able to identify all of the options. You may see things in somewhat stark, black-and-white terms. It often helps to talk to someone you trust, because he or she may help you look at things more objectively.)

3. Think through the positive and negative consequences of each option.
   Positive: If Ira found his birth family and they welcomed him warmly, he might have a sense of completion and end up with two loving families. That would be great.
   Negative: If his birth parents did not welcome him, he might experience strong feelings of rejection. If they had problems—if they were drug addicts, for instance—he might also have a strong emotional reaction.
      The negative consequences—that sort of knowledge or rejection—might be hard for Ira to deal with at this stage of his life but might be easier a few years down the road, when he possesses a greater level of personal maturity. And if Ira didn't search for his birth parents at all, he might have some unanswered questions but would still have his loving and supportive adoptive family.
4. Weigh your options in light of your values and goals. Ira knows that his parents think he should wait until he is an adult before searching for his birth parents. He thinks there are some things he could do now, based on the knowledge he has, but to do so behind his parents' back would be against his (and their) values of honesty and openness with family members.

5. Make a decision. Ira knows he wouldn't feel good about searching for his birth family secretly. At this point, with so much else going on in his life—upcoming SATs, drama, new friends, and a new girlfriend—he has decided to hold off on a formal search. But he has reviewed everything his parents have given him and told him to date, and he has started a list of search resources and ideas as they come to him so that he will be prepared when and if he decides to further investigate.

If you are considering an important decision in your life, keep in mind that if the decision you have made requires some form of action, it will require proper planning. Or, it could be that like Ira, you may have specifically chosen not to take action in a particular situation. Whatever your decision, it will be important to make it known to the people you are close to, particularly if the choice you have made involves them in some way. As always, remember the importance of effective communication.

Often only time and hindsight will tell if you made the right decision. The most you can ask of yourself is that you make your decisions as carefully and responsibly as you can.

Making a Commitment

Although every decision you make requires time and energy, some choices have higher stakes than others. At some point in your life you may be romantically involved with someone. When and if this happens, keep in mind that one of the biggest decisions you can make is whether to enter a committed relationship with that person. Marriage or cohabitation is a big step. It means blending your spaces, cultures, families, finances, and plans for the future. A successful relationship requires a high level of emotional maturity because there are many compromises and personal sacrifices involved. Love, while essential, isn't always enough. As you learned in Chapter Three, divorces and breakups can be painful. That's why it's worthwhile to consider your decision carefully.

Here are some things to think about and do before you make a commitment. They are adapted from *The Intermarriage Handbook,* by Judy Petsonk and Jim Remson.

1. Try to assess your compatibility regarding certain issues that will almost certainly arise after you move in together. Talk with your prospective partner about his or her attitudes to money and sex, for instance. Talk about your plans regarding children and explore your attitudes toward child rearing and discipline. Baby-sit together. Go window shopping for furniture. Shop for groceries together. How do his or her attitudes and tastes mesh with yours?

2. Assess your cultural differences. If you come from different cultures, celebrate each other's holidays. Discuss how cultural values may come into everyday life—such as the way you each display emotion and affection; the way you dress; your expectations regarding housekeeping, sex, and child rearing, if you plan to have kids together.

3. Meet and get to know each other's families. Observe how your prospective partner's family members relate to one another. Are there any things that you really enjoy or are bothered by?

4. Explore your own ethnic, cultural, and spiritual beliefs, values, and goals. Do you, for instance, believe in God? How do you practice or demonstrate your faith? If you plan to have children, how would you like to raise them? Now find out how your prospective partner views these issues. Does he or she respect your beliefs and values? Can you find acceptable middle ground?

5. Inform yourself. If the two of you come from different backgrounds—racial, cultural, ethnic, or religious—try to learn as much as you can about your loved one's background. You can talk to members of his or her family. Try to find out, too, what it is like to live in a

mixed family of the kind you are thinking of starting. Seek out couples who have done it. Talk to them about the positive and negative sides of their experience. If their relationship has worked and survived hardship, find out how they have handled the various issues that have arisen. Remember, too, that you can also celebrate your cultural differences and use them to expand and enrich your lives.

6. Confront your own prejudices. This is particularly important if you are entering into a mixed relationship of any kind. Ask yourself if, deep down, you hold any negative stereotypes regarding the racial, religious, or cultural group to which your prospective partner belongs. Where did they originate? Have you, or can you, truly move past them? Learning more about your loved one's background may help you to overcome any lingering prejudice. Otherwise, it could cause problems in your future relationship.

7. Negotiate some issues. Consciously think of some areas where you and your potential partner differ, and try to negotiate them. The steps involved in negotiation are much like those involved in conflict resolution that you learned in chapter 2.

   • Define the issue to be resolved.
   • Explore how each of you views the issue.
   • Try to understand your partner's point of view.
   • Use effective communication techniques ("I" messages, active listening).
   • Focus on needs, not just the outcome you desire. Acknowledge each other's feelings.
   • Brainstorm possible solutions.
   • Choose one that allows you both to win.
   • Discuss how you might later evaluate your chosen solution.

   As important as negotiation is, you should also be aware of the fact that there are some differences that you won't be able to resolve. Sometimes you and your partner will just have to live with differences. As difficult as that may sound, know that everyone involved in a committed relationship has had to learn how to do this.

8. Practice your solutions. If, for instance, you have decided, after talking and negotiating, to divide your holidays between your respective families, do it. See if and how it actually works.

9. Assess outside pressures. Do your family and close friends disapprove of your relationship? Do you have the strength to deal with disapproval? How do you and your prospective partner handle stress?

10. Listen to your own doubts. List some of your fears or doubts about the relationship and talk them over with your loved one. Explore how you might handle some of these problems. Try to determine whether or not your fears are realistic. If people you respect express fears and doubts, listen to them and try to evaluate them in the same way.

11. If it is available, take a class that explores some of these issues. Many religious denominations require engaged couples to take a premarriage class or counseling before their wedding. Try to find such a class in your community.

By working through some of these issues, you may gain even greater confidence that you have met the right person. On the other hand, you may decide that your differences are too great. Or you may simply pinpoint areas in your relationship that need work. Remember that personal and cultural differences between partners in a relationship can be constructive. They can stimulate personal growth for each individual. In that case, they are to be celebrated. If they lead to undue stress or conflict, though, you may want to think twice before making a commitment to that person. Ultimately, the choice of whether to enter into a commitment with another person is one that only you and your partner can make. And of course sometimes mistakes are made, and committed relationships fail. Every responsible decision has a risk involved. Be sure to make your decision wisely and knowledgeably.

Becoming a Parent

Deciding when and if to have children is another very big life choice. Caring for a child can be joyous, but it is a full-time, demanding job. Once you have a child, you will be legally responsible for raising him or her until the age of 18 (21 in some states). This applies to unmarried fathers, as well as mothers. Beyond providing the basics of food, clothing, and shelter, parenthood means nursing children through illness, offering emotional support, providing discipline, setting limits, and often putting children's needs before your own. Needless to say, it is a huge commitment. Again, a very high level of emotional maturity is required.

Some people are very certain about their desire to become parents. The only question for them is when. Others are less certain. Many teenagers, in particular, may not be ready to make a final decision on parenthood. Some people don't decide that they want children until they are in their 30s or 40s and have established careers for themselves. This trend is more common today than ever before. Advances in reproductive technology have made it possible for women to have children at later ages.

Some families today make a decision not to have children. Again, it may be too early for most teenagers to make a final decision in that regard, but it is important to remember that parenthood isn't for everybody.

Here are some of the questions you can ask yourself in the course of deciding whether or not to have children.

- Do I like children?
- Do I have the financial resources to support them?
- Is my relationship with my partner healthy?

- Do my partner and I share common views regarding child rearing, including discipline and setting limits? Do we know how to communicate effectively and work through our differences?
- What sort of outside support systems do I/we have, from extended family members and in our community?
- How would having a child affect other life goals and plans?

If you aren't certain about your desire to have a child, or if you don't want one any time soon, keep in mind that the only sure way to avoid an unwanted pregnancy is to abstain from sex. When and if you do decide to become sexually active, you should use a reliable contraceptive technique. A doctor or family planning center, which you can locate through the Yellow Pages of your telephone book, can give you information regarding contraception. (See chapter 6 for suggested reading in this regard.)

Getting There: Meeting Your Goals

Can you achieve your goals? Of course you can. Even young people growing up in the most dysfunctional family situations can grow up to be happy, healthy adults. Recent psychological research shows that many children from backgrounds involving abuse, poverty, alcohol, drugs, criminality, mental illness, and war grow up to be competent, reasonably untroubled adults. That does not mean that they have been unscarred by their troubled childhoods, but they have moved past them and have not been crippled by them.

Finding Strength in Yourself: Becoming Resilient

People who have moved on from dysfunctional families to happy, healthy lives are said to be "resilient." They have developed strength in the face of adversity and that helps them to develop strategies to move on. Resilience is a relatively new area of research for psychologists, but the good news is that it seems anyone can learn how to practice it. Writing in the May/June 1998 issue of *Psychology Today,* Debra Blum summarizes some of the current research about resilience. Resilient people, it seems, share the following characteristics.

- They have faith in a higher power or in themselves and in their own futures. Faith helps people perceive bad times as temporary and gives them the optimism and strength to weather them.
- They get outside help when needed. Resilient people often find help in resolving their problems from within their own families—from grandparents or other relatives. When they can't, they find it outside their families.
- They set goals and plan for the future.
- They believe in themselves and appreciate their own abilities and strengths, including their humor, creativity, independence, and initiative.
- They often develop and recognize strategies for getting through difficult times. A teenager who is abused, for instance, might find an escape in books and imagination—they just take her somewhere else, away from her troubles for at least a brief time. Someone else might turn to music.

How can you develop these qualities in yourself? You have already learned about the importance of identifying your values and setting goals. While faith in a higher being is an intensely personal quality, you can develop faith in yourself and your future by allowing yourself to dream and moving toward your dreams and goals by simply staying in school. You can work on your self-image and self-esteem by affirming your own worth and focusing on things you enjoy and are good at. That will also offer you an escape, if one is needed, from current troubles. Marcy finds that she relaxes when focusing on photography. The creative process makes her forget about problems at home. And she's starting to really acknowledge her talent for taking pictures. A lot of people can learn the skill, but not everyone can take an ordinary scene and turn it into art.

Finally, you can reach out for help in meeting your goals. Few people can meet all of life's challenges alone, whether or not they are facing personal crises. Healthy families can be great sources of support. Mentors and role models can both supplement family support and fill certain voids. And there are other helpful community resources as well, as you're about to find out.

Role Models and Mentors

A positive role model is someone—known or unknown to you—who demonstrates positive behavior and in so doing demonstrates values you respect. In that way—through actions—he or she teaches valuable life skills. Ira's mother, for instance, undertakes a daily balancing act between career and home, keeping her cool and somehow managing to succeed in one area without neglecting the other or herself. Simply by observing her, Ira is learning how she does it. Eli likes the way Mr. Tyler treats each of the young people who work for him. He doesn't just give them orders but demonstrates patience in teaching them new skills and giving them time to master what they have learned. He also shows concern for their futures, asking them about their plans and offering encouragement. By observing him, Eli is learning the value of patience, empathy, and support. Mr. Tyler's interest in his employees earns him their respect, loyalty, and hard work.

Whenever you are drawn to someone as a role model, ask yourself what it is that you admire. Do they demonstrate confidence in themselves? Can you tell, through their behavior, what matters to them? Remember that you can gain inspiration from celebrities and sports figures, but in coping with day-to-day issues, you shouldn't overlook the role models who are closer to home.

Role models can also be mentors, but the two are somewhat different. A mentor is a respected adult with whom a young person has a one-on-one, ongoing relationship. A mentor will take an active interest in a young person's life, offering support and guidance through good, as well as stressful, times.

Sometimes mentors enter a young person's life for a specific purpose—to offer help with school work, or career plans, for instance. You may be lucky enough to find more than one mentor for yourself at a given time. But as a rule, a mentor will be someone with whom you have an ongoing relationship, who shares and demonstrates his or her values, someone with whom you communicate easily and effectively and whom you trust to offer sound guidance and advice.

Mentors, like role models, can be found close to home. If you greatly admire a parent, caregiver, or family friend, for example, you may also consider him or her a mentor. Eli had a mentor in his grandfather. It is a bit early to tell, but he may find another in Mr. Tyler. Mentoring relationships can evolve if you are open to the interest a respected and trusted adult takes in your life. You can also actively recruit a mentor by approaching someone with a direct request to take on the role. It may sound scary, but the rewards can be great.

There are many organizations that match young people with mentors. Big Brothers/Big Sisters is one such well-established organization that matches carefully screened adults with children and teenagers, based on interests, ages, and needs (see chapter 6 for contact information). Many "little brothers" and "little sisters" come from homes where there is no parent of the child's sex with whom the young person can interact. By a little brother spending time with a big brother or a little sister spending time with a big sister—going bowling or to the movies, or just hanging out at home—these young people can gain a perspective that may be missing at home.

In addition, there are now mentoring programs that offer assistance with various areas of family life. Programs exist in most communities to pair parents of newborns with experienced parents to help them through the confusing first days, weeks, and months of their child's life. In some areas, young, unmarried fathers who wish to be involved in their children's lives can be matched with older men who can teach them positive fathering skills, if they have not been exposed to that role previously. Many religious groups match newlyweds with couples married for many years who can share their experiences and in that way help young couples work through the inevitable ups and downs of married life. The message is clear: If you reach out, help is available.

Resolving Issues

In order to move on with your life and work on meeting your goals, it may be necessary to resolve certain situations from your past. It was important, for example, for Marcy to work on issues related to anger and communication. Otherwise, she might well have encountered these problems in future relationships.

Sometimes you can work on these issues by yourself or with the help of a family member or friend. In other cases, you may need some outside assistance. There are many resources in your community to help you work through these situations and even to help clarify your goals.

Counselors

A counselor can help you identify the issues and develop a plan for dealing with them constructively, if more help is needed. He or she can direct you toward other forms of help, such as peer support groups and self-help groups. A family doctor, school counselor, or religious leader can help you in this regard. Or you can call a hot line—such as a youth crisis line—and receive direction.

Therapists

Therapists are usually psychologists or social workers, trained to help you work through emotional problems. These may involve family issues, eating disorders, or problems with self-image. A therapist can help you identify the root causes of the problem and assist you in reaching a solution. They can also help you identify strengths or self-defeating behavior and attitudes that you may be overlooking.

Group therapy, as opposed to individual therapy, involves a group of people who meet to discuss and work through similar issues, guided by a therapist. Family therapy, as you learned in Chapter Three, involves a whole family meeting to discuss and work through ongoing family problems, with the therapist serving as a mediator and guide.

The relationship between a therapist and client requires a high level of trust and respect, given the intimate nature of the problems being discussed. To find a competent therapist, ask a counselor, doctor, trusted adult, or professional body, such as the American Psychological Association (APA) for several referrals. (See Chapter Six for contact information.) By telephone, ask each about their credentials and experience with situations like yours. Ask for some guidelines as to how each therapist might deal with your situation. Ask them to identify the relevant licensing body in your state, and check their credentials. After your first meeting with a therapist, assess how comfortable you felt with that person. Don't expect a therapist to offer easy solutions or to tell you things you want to hear, but ask yourself if you were treated with respect and if the therapist showed genuine concern for your well-being. Do not continue to see a therapist if you do not feel comfortable with him or her in any way.

Peer support groups

These are forums where teenagers coping with similar situations, experiences, and problems get together to share their stories and coping strategies. Sometimes these groups have an adult leader who helps to direct the conversation.

You can get a referral to a support group from a counselor or hot line in your community. You can also look for advertisements in community newspapers and at community centers. The local library and the self-help clearinghouses, which you can look up on the Internet, can also help you find a group.

The best way to get help from a support group is to become an active participant. It may take you a while to speak up, but once you become comfortable in the group, chances are you'll feel OK about sharing your story. In the meantime, you can help others to share their experiences by being an active listener. And respect the confidentiality of the group. The personal and private stories you hear in your peer support group should not be repeated to outsiders.

Self-help groups

These are much like support groups, in that they bring people with common problems together to share their stories and coping strategies. Many self-help groups are part of a wider network of such groups and adhere to a common philosophy. Alateen, for instance, is an offshoot of Al-Anon and Alcoholics Anonymous. They all adhere to a 12-step philosophy. You can find out more information about AA, Al-Anon, and Alateen by checking their web sites or calling them (see Chapter Six for contact information).

Educate Yourself

Even if you do not currently face a difficult personal decision and even if you are not (and certainly if you are) at an important crossroads in your life, it's pretty easy to learn more about the necessary life skills that can help you during these times. The self-help section of your local library is full of books with advice on all areas of family life. In addition, classes are available in most communities on many subjects that are directly related to family life. Relevant classes might include the following:

- Effective communication and conflict resolution. As you have learned, effective communication and conflict resolution skills are two of the cornerstones of healthy relationships.
- Family planning. Whether or not you have decided that you would like to be a parent someday, a family planning workshop can educate you regarding birth control, fertility, infertility, and adoption options, among other issues. This is useful well in advance of becoming sexually active in any way.
- Child development and parenting skills. If you have decided that you would like to be a parent, learn about what is really involved in caring for an infant and raising a child. Don't wait until you are actually expecting a child to find out what might be involved.
- Personal financial management. A basic course might teach you about budgeting for yourself and a family. You would learn how to live on what you earn. You would also learn how to balance a checkbook and the ins and outs of credit. You might also want to learn about investment and planning for the future, for such things as buying a home, saving for an education (for you or your children), and planning for retirement.

Creating a Sense of Family

Since Lin has moved in, Annie has met all kinds of new people. She seems to have really interesting friends, both men and women, from all walks of life. Many, though not all, are lesbians or gay men. Annie notices, however, that she has never met any of Lin's relatives, even though they live across town. One day, Annie screws up the courage to ask Lin about her family. "My mother died a few years back. We were pretty close," Lin said slowly. "And my dad, well, he's never had much use for homosexuals. After mom died, he told me that he couldn't accept my 'sick lifestyle.' He just put up with it for mom's sake. My sister agreed with him, so I don't see much of them anymore. That's why my friends are so important to me. And now I have you and Lisa and your mom. You're my family too."

More than other groups perhaps, lesbians and gay men have learned the importance of developing their own sense of family. That's partly because a significant number may have been rejected by their families after they came out. But they aren't the only ones to choose a definition of family that depends more on the quality of the relationships involved than blood ties.

In her book *In Praise of Single Parents*, Shoshana Alexander writes of finding a sense of family for herself and her young son through shared housing. Sharing a home with several other unrelated adults gave her son a community of caring adults, male and female, and provided Alexander with the support and backup she might otherwise find from a partner.

College students often form close, lifelong bonds with classmates and roommates, often the result of sharing the experience of being away from home for the first time. Certain immigrant groups have traditionally identified a familylike bond with among compatriots living together outside their country of origin. New arrivals may be offered the benefits of being "like family," such as a place to sleep and a regular spot around the dinner table.

Even if they have loving parents and caregivers and full extended families, all children can benefit from the extra love "honorary" aunts and uncles can provide. Couples can use close friends to support them individually and in their relationship, as siblings might. This is particularly true given the mobility of today's society, where biological and adoptive family members might live thousands of miles away from one another. Single adults, who may feel no need for a committed romantic partnership, often find genuine satisfaction in the relationships they have built with people in their communities.

Building these ties takes time, openness to a wider definition of "family," and initiative. Like Shoshana Alexander, you may find it through sharing accommodations with other people. You may stumble into it out of necessity after leaving home. Try inviting friends and acquaintances over for a potluck holiday dinner, an event that is often associated with "family." You can also meet like-minded people through your house of worship, in classes, and through community organizations.

A Family of Your Own

The face of today's family has changed dramatically over the past 50 years and is likely to continue evolving over the next century. And with the changing tide, attitudes are becoming more accepting as well. Forty years ago a family like Ira's or Annie's might have been the subject of discussion among disapproving neighbors. But today, a growing number of people are familiar with these kinds of contemporary families and don't give them a second thought. And many, of course, are members of nontraditional families themselves.

The members of today's families are all breaking new ground, in different ways. People who are in what was once known as nuclear families are seeing the roles of family members change. Today, it is as acceptable for a woman to be in the workforce and as involved in her career as her husband is. Many of these women choose to have children later in life or are managing to work and have children at the same time.

Then there are women who are choosing to have children without getting married, and couples who are opting not to have children. There are families whose members come from different cultural, religious, and racial backgrounds; families headed by homosexual parents; families living with (and sometimes headed by) extended family members, such as grandparents, uncles, aunts, and cousins; and blended families, where members of two separate families come together to form a new one.

Ultimately, what matters much more is not the composition of a given family but the way in which its members interact. As you know by now, a healthy family treats its members with compassion, empathy, love, and respect. As important, family members take the time to talk and to listen to one another. In this way they are able to enjoy happy times and to survive hard ones by relying on one another.

It's important to remember that there is no such thing as a perfect family. Even those that may seem happy and flawless all have situations and issues to contend with. And since all family members are human, they all make mistakes. There will be times that they forget to listen and to communicate, and when they don't treat one another with the kindness they deserve.

On the other hand, there are families that don't function in a healthy way most of the time and that don't provide the basic needs for its members. People who are in a dysfunctional family can sometimes work together to improve life for themselves and for the other members by learning to cope with anger and to communicate more effectively.

If you are unhappy in your family and don't think life will improve for you until you are old enough to move away, remember that ultimately you can do this and start a healthy and thriving family of your own. At the same time, keep in mind that being a member of any kind of healthy family, whether nuclear or nontraditional, takes a lot of patience and commitment, as well as the ability to accept the differences and imperfections of those you live with. Once you do that, you can begin to cherish and celebrate the gifts of being with people who, regardless of their differences, share the ability to communicate effectively. It is that quality, above all, that makes any type of family a healthy one.

6

Where to Find Help

Adoption

The following resources provide information on adoption.

National Adoption Information Clearinghouse
330 C Street SW
Washington, DC 20447
Telephone: 888-251-0075
703-352-3488
Fax: 703-385-3206
E-mail: naic@calib.com
Web: http://www.calib.com/naic/
This service of the Children's Bureau, U.S. Department of Health and Human Services, provides fact sheets, articles, and other information about all areas of adoption, and a directory of adoption agencies and resources.

Pact, An Adoption Alliance
3450 Sacramento Street, Suite 239
San Francisco, CA 94118
Telephone: 415-221-6957
E-mail: info@pactadopt.org
Web: http://www.pactadopt.org
Pact provides information to adopted children of color and to adoptive and biological parents, and publishes *Pact Press*, which addresses issues for families with adopted children of color.

Child Abuse and Domestic Violence

The following resources provide help and information for teenagers coping with any form of abuse or violence at home.

National Child Abuse Hot Line (Childhelp USA)
Telephone: 800-422-4453
To report abuse and to obtain literature and referrals to help, call this confidential hot line. Assistance is available in English and Spanish 24 hours a day.

National Clearinghouse on Child Abuse
  and Neglect Information
330 C Street SW
Washington, DC 20447
Telephone: 800-394-3366
703-385-7565
Fax: 703-385-3206
E-mail: nccanch@calib.com
Web: http://www.calib.com/nccanch/
This clearinghouse provides information and resources on the prevention of child abuse and neglect.

National Committee to Prevent Child Abuse
200 South Michigan Avenue, 17th Floor
Chicago, IL 60604-4357
Telephone: 312-663-3520
800-556-2722
Fax: 312-939-8962
Web: http://www.childabuse.org
This organization provides information about child abuse and parenting skills, focusing on prevention of child abuse through parenting education. It maintains local chapters throughout the United States. Extensive on-line information includes the Youth Focus site, with information regarding hot lines, abusive situations, and nonviolent conflict resolution.

National Council on Child Abuse and Family Violence
1155 Connecticut Avenue NW, Suite 400
Washington, DC 20036
Telephone: 202-429-6695
800-222-2000
The council provides information about spouse, child, and elder abuse, as well as referrals, through a toll-free help line.

National Hot Line on Domestic Violence
Telephone: 800-799-7233
800-787-3224 (TDD for hearing impaired)
This hot line handles calls regarding domestic violence 24 hours a day and on a confidential basis.

Parents Anonymous—The National Organization
675 West Foothill Boulevard, Suite 220
Claremont, CA 91711-3475
Telephone: 909-621-6184
This international organization, with local chapters throughout North America, is dedicated to parenting education and provides information and support for parents who fear they might abuse children, helping them to cope without losing control.

Family Planning and Parenting

The following resources provide information on sexuality, family planning, and parenting.

National Black Child Development Institute
1023 15th Street, N.W.
Suite 600
Washington, DC 20005
Telephone: 202-387-1281
Fax: 202-234-1738
E-mail: moreinfo@nbcdi.org
Web: http://www.nbcdi.org
This organization offers information and pamphlets on a variety of topics, including parenting, public policy and child health care.

National Center for Fathering
P.O. Box 413888
Kansas City, MO 64141
Telephone: 800-593-3237
Fax: 913-384-4665
Web: http://www.fathers.com
This source provides practical information for fathers and publishes *Today's Father* magazine.

Planned Parenthood Federation of America
810 Seventh Avenue
New York, NY 10019
Telephone: 212-541-7800
800-230-7526 (to reach a local center)
Fax: 212-245-1845
E-mail: communications@ppfa.org
Web: http://www.plannedparenthood.org/

Planned Parenthood provides sexual and reproductive health information and health care services, and maintains clinics throughout the United States and local chapters throughout North America.

Sexuality Information and Education
   Council of the United States (SIECUS)
130 West 42nd Street, Suite 350
New York, NY 10036-7802
Telephone: 212-819-9770
Fax: 212-819-9776
E-mail: siecus@siecus.org
Web: http://www.seicus.org
This contact offers information and comprehensive education about sexuality.

Zero to Three National Center for Infants, Toddlers
   and Families
734 15th Street NW, Suite 1000
Washington, DC 20005
Telephone: 202-638-1144
Fax: 202-638-0851
E-mail: 0to3@zerotothree.org
Web: http://www.zerotothree.org
This is a national organization dedicated to advancing the healthy development of infants and toddlers. Zero to Three offers parenting tips and publications and maintains the Early Head Start National Resource Center, located online at http://www.ehsnrc.org. This site contains information on parenting and early childhood development.

Family Situations

The following resources provide general or specific information about various family-related issues.

Parents Without Partners
401 North Michigan Avenue
Chicago, IL 60611-4267
Telephone: 800-637-7974
Primarily a nationwide support organization for parents, many local chapters also maintain activities for the children of members.

The Sibling Support Project
Children's Hospital and Medical Center
P.O. Box 5371, CL-09
Seattle, WA 98105-0371
Telephone: 206-368-4911
Fax: 206-368-4816
E-mail: dmeyer@chmc.org
Web http://www.chmc.org/departmt/sibsupp
This national program serving the interests of brothers and sisters of people with special health and developmental needs can provide links to local peer-support groups, as well as information and e-mail bulletin boards (SibKids and SibNet) for siblings of all ages.

Stepfamily Association of America
650 J Street, Suite 205
Lincoln, NE 68508
Telephone: 402-477-7837
800-735-0329
This organization provides information, education, and support for stepfamilies.

Getting Help

The following organizations can provide information about and referrals to self-help groups and counseling, therapy, and mental health professionals in your area.

American Academy of Child and Adolescent Psychiatry
3615 Wisconsin Avenue NW
Washington, DC 20016-3007
Telephone: 202-966-7300
Fax: 202-966-2891
Web: http://www.aacap.org
This association can offer referrals to psychiatrists who specialize in working with young people.

American Association for Marriage and Family Therapists
1100 17th Street NW, 10th Floor
Washington, DC 20036
Telephone: 800-374-2638
Web: http://www.aamft.org
This organization offers referrals to family therapists within the United States and Canada. AAMFT also publishes a referral directory that is available online.

American Psychological Association
750 First Street NE
Washington, DC 20002-4242
Telephone: 202-336-5700
E-mail: public.affairs@apa.org
Web: http://www.apa.org
This national association of professional psychologists offers information and referrals to practicing psychologists and state psychological associations.

American Self-Help Clearinghouse
Northwest Covenant Medical Center
Denville, NJ 07834-2995
Telephone: 973-625-3037/ TTY 625-9853
Web: http://www.cmhc.com/selfhelp
This on-line self-help sourcebook lists organizations that can help people find and/or start support groups in their communities (or online). Toll free numbers are also listed.

National Association of Social Workers
750 First Street NE, Suite 700
Washington, DC 20002
Telephone: 202-408-8600/ TTP 202-408-8396
Fax: 202-336-8311
Web: http://www.naswdc.org
This professional organization offers referrals to clinical social workers around the country.

National Self-Help Clearinghouse
25 West 43rd Street, Suite 620
New York, NY 10036
Telephone: 212-354-8525
This clearinghouse refers callers to appropriate regional clearinghouses and self-help organizations.

Grief and Loss

The following resources provide information and referrals for those coping with grief and loss.

The Compassionate Friends
P.O. Box 3696
Oak Brook, IL 60522-3696
Telephone: 630-990-0010
E-mail: tcf_national@prodigy.com
Providing information and connecting bereaved parents and siblings to support groups throughout North America, this organization is specifically for families who have lost a child.

Grief Recovery Helpline
Telephone: 800-445-4808 (in United States; 9 A.M. to 5 P.M., Pacific time)
800-916-3224 (in Canada; 9 A.M. to 5 P.M. Eastern time)
Trained grief recovery counselors take calls.

Rainbows
1111 Tower Road
Schaumberg, IL 60173
Telephone: 800-266-3206
Teenagers and adults who are experiencing loss through death or divorce are connected to peer support groups throughout North America.

Homosexuality

The following resources provide information to families with homosexual parents or children.

Canadian Gay, Lesbian and Bisexual Resource Directory
386 Montrose Street
Winnipeg, Manitoba, Canada
Telephone: 204-488-1805
800-245-2734
E-mail: cglbrd@cglbrd.com
Web: http://www.cglbrd.com/
This directory of Canadian resources includes connections to gay and lesbian youth services and family and parent information.

Children of Lesbians and Gays Everywhere (COLAGE)
3543 18th Street, Suite 17
San Francisco, CA 94110
Telephone: 415-861-5437
Fax: 415-255-8345
E-mail: colage@colage.org
Web: http://www.colage.org
COLAGE supports and advocates for children of lesbian, gay, bisexual, and transgendered parents and their families. It has 20 affiliates across North America that run various groups for young people of different ages and interests. Most have some support, discussion, and/or social groups to connect children

of gay, lesbian, bisexual, or transgender parents. Nationally, COLAGE has two e-mail discussion or chat lists, one for teens older than 14 and another for younger children.

Gay and Lesbian National Hotline: 888-843-4564
Web: http://www.glnh.org
This help line offers peer counseling, information and refer-rals for gays and lesbians, Monday-Friday, 6 P.M. to 11 P.M. (Eastern time)

Parents and Friends of Lesbians and Gays (PFLAG)
1101 14th Street NW, Suite 1030
Washington, DC 20005
Telephone: 202-638-4200
Web: http://www.pflag.org
PFLAG offers support and information for families with gay, lesbian, and bisexual children and also advocates gay and lesbian rights. In addition, it promotes public education and publishes the *Be Yourself* pamphlet of questions and an-swers for lesbian, gay, and bisexual youth. Local chapters are maintained throughout North America.

Mentors and Role Models

The following resources provide information for those interested in seeking or becoming a mentor.

Big Brothers/Big Sisters of America
230 North 13th Street
Philadelphia, PA 19107
Telephone: 215-567-7000
E-mail: national@bbbsa.org
Web: http://www.bbbsa.org
Children and teenagers are matched up with carefully screened adults for an ongoing, one-to-one mentoring relationship.

Big Brothers and Big Sisters of Canada
3228 South Service Road
Suite 113E
Burlington, Ontario, Canada L7N 3H8
Telephone: 800-263-9133
E-mail: mmcknight@bbsc.ca
Web: http://www.bbsc.ca
Children and teenagers are matched up with carefully screened adults for an ongoing one-to-one mentoring relationship.

Boys and Girls Clubs of America
1230 West Peachtree Street NW
Atlanta, GA 30309-3447
Telephone: 800-815-5700
Web: http://www.bgca.org
This national organization puts young people in touch with clubs in their area. (For automatic referral line, call 800-854-2582). Most BGCA core programs, in areas such as character and leadership, health and lifeskills, and sports and fitness, involve a mentoring component and contact with caring peers and adults.

Boys and Girls Clubs of Canada
Suite 703
7030 Woodbine Avenue
Markham, Ontario, Canada L3R 6G2
Telephone: 905-477-7272
Fax: 905-477-2056
This national organization offers referrals to local clubs throughout Canada, many of which offer mentoring and peer mediation programs.

Peer Resources
1052 Davie Street
Victoria, BC, Canada V8S 4E3
Telephone: 800-567-3700

Fax: 250-595-3504
E-mail: rcarr@islandnet.com
Web: http://www.peer.ca
This organization lists peer mentoring programs for youth
and adults throughout Canada and the United States.

Runaways

The following hot lines provide help for teens who are
thinking of running away from home or who already have.

Boys Town National Hot Line
Telephone: 800-448-3000
Calls from Canada are welcome to this hot line for teens
in crisis.

Canadian Kids' Help Phone Crisis Line
Telephone: 800-668-6868
Web: http://kidshelp.sympatico.ca
This 24-hour service puts young people in touch with
professional counselors who will deal with any issue,
including family problems, sexuality, drug abuse, sexual
violence, and suicide. Web site is designed to ease access
to information and supplement telephone service. Services
are available in English or French.

Covenant House Nineline
Telephone: 800-999-9999
This hot line is for teens who are thinking about running
away or runaways who want to send messages home.

Runaway Hot Line/National Runaway Switchboard
Telephone: 800-621-4000
This 24-hour, toll-free hot line serves teenagers who are
thinking about running away or already have run away from

home, and their families. It provides counseling and message services for youth and families.

Substance Abuse and Codependence

The following resources provide help and information
for those teenagers coping with substance abuse and/or
codependency.

Alateen and Al-Anon Family Group Headquarters
1600 Corporate Landing Parkway
Virginia Beach, VA 23454-5617
Telephone: 800-344-2666 (hot line)
757-563-1600
800-443-4525 (in Canada)
Fax: 757-563-1655
Web: http://www.al-anon.alateen.org
This is a self-help organization for teens whose lives have been
affected by a family member's problem drinking. Referrals are
available to local chapters throughout North America.

Co-Dependents Anonymous (CoDA)
P.O. Box 33577
Phoenix, AZ 85067-3577
Telephone: 602-277-7991
E-mail: info@ourcoda.org
This is a 12-step self-help program for recovery from code-
pendence. CoDa has chapters throughout North America.

Nar-a-Teen and Nar-Anon Family Groups
P.O. Box 2562
Palos Verdes Peninsula, CA 90274
Telephone: 213-547-5800
This is a self-help organization for teens whose lives have

been affected by a family member's drug problem. Referrals are available to local chapters throughout North America.

National Clearinghouse for Alcohol and Drug Information (NCADI)
P.O. Box 2345
Rockville, MD 20852
Telephone: 800-729-6686
800-487-4889 (TDD for hearing impaired)
NCADI, the information service of the Center for Substance Abuse and Prevention of the U.S. Department of Health and Human Services, provides current information and materials about alcohol and other drugs.

National Council on Alcoholism and Drug Dependence (NCADD)
12 West 21st Street
New York, NY 10010
Telephone: 800-622-2255 (24 hours/day)
The NCADD Hopeline will refer callers to a local affiliate office and can also provide information on alcohol and other drug abuse, support, and some treatment referral.

National Council on Codependence, Inc.
P.O. Box 40095
Phoenix, AZ 85067-0095
Telephone: 602-735-6870
E-mail: guideline@bitsmart.com
Web: http://nccod.netgate.net
The council offers information on codependence and referrals to treatment facilities and professionals.

Further Reading

Alexander, Shoshana. *In Praise of Single Parents*. New York: Houghton Mifflin, 1994.

Berry, Dawn Bradley. *The Domestic Violence Sourcebook*. Los Angeles: Lowell House, 1996.

Brewster, Susan. *To Be an Anchor in the Storm: A Guide for Families and Friends of Abused Women*. New York: Ballantine Books, 1997.

Coontz, Stephanie. *The Way We Really Are*. New York: Basic Books, 1997.

Dentemaro, Christine, and Rachel Kranz. *Straight Talk About Anger*. New York: Facts On File, 1995.

Edelson, Paula. *Straight Talk About Teenage Pregnancy*. New York. Facts On File, 1999.

Funderburg, Lise. *Black, White, Other: Biracial Americans Talk About Race and Identity*. New York: William Morrow, 1994.

Grollman, Earl A. *Straight Talk About Death for Teenagers: How to Cope with Losing Someone You Love*. Boston: Beacon Press, 1993.

Hyde, Margaret O. *Know About Abuse*. New York: Walker and Company, 1992.

Kaeser, Gigi, and Peggy Gillespie. *Of Many Colors: Portraits of Multiracial Families*. Amherst: University of Massachusetts Press, 1997.

Krementz, Jill. *How It Feels to Be Adopted*. New York: Alfred A. Knopf, 1982.

———. *How It Feels When Parents Divorce*. New York: Alfred A. Knopf, 1988.

Leder, Jane Mersky. *Brothers and Sisters: How They Shape Our Lives*. New York: St. Martin's Press, 1991.

Levy, Barrie. *In Love and in Danger: A Teen's Guide to Breaking Free of Abusive Relationships*. Seattle: Seal Press, 1993.

Meyer, Donald J., and Patricia F. Vadasy. *Sibshops: Workshops for Brothers and Sisters of Children with Special Needs.* Baltimore: Paul H. Brooks, 1994.

————. *Living with a Brother or Sister with Special Needs: A Book for Sibs.* 2d ed. Seattle: University of Washington Press, 1996.

Nash, Renea D. *Coping as a Biracial/Biethnic Teen.* New York: Rosen Publishing Group, 1995.

NiCarthy, Ginny. *Getting Free: You Can End Abuse and Take Back Your Life.* 3d. ed. Seattle: Seal Press, 1986.

Petsonk, Judy, and Jim Remsen. *The Intermarriage Handbook.* New York: William Morrow, 1988.

Rubin, Jeffrey, and Carol Rubin. *When Families Fight: How to Handle Conflict with Those You Love.* New York: William Morrow, 1989.

Ryan, Elizabeth A. *Straight Talk About Parents.* New York: Facts On File, 1989.

Steinberg, Laurence, and Ann Levine. *You and Your Adolescent.* New York: HarperCollins, 1997.

INDEX

A

abandonment 47–48
abuse and neglect 62, 75–88
   abuser characteristics 87–88
   common types 76–77
   cycle of 63–64, 77, 79, 87–88
   effects of 78–81
   healing wounds of 86–88
   mismanaged anger and 66, 77, 87
   motivations for 77–78
   resiliency and 103–4
   stopping 81–86
   substance abuse and 69–71, 72,
     75, 77–78
acceptance 42
achievement, pressure for 31–32
active listening 19–20, 69
addiction *see* substance dependence
adoption 33–37
   and birth-parent search 33–34, 35,
     96–98
   and early emotional neglect 80–81
   second-parent 7
   single-mother 5
   transracial 1, 9–10, 15–16, 34,
     35–37, 43–44
Adoption 2002 10
adult caregivers 22-26 *see also* family;
  parenthood; *specific family types*
adult resources 47–48, 37, 105–7
affectionate care 80–81
aggressive behavior 66, 68, 70, 79
Al-Anon 72–73, 109
Alateen 73, 90, 109
alcohol abuse *see* substance
  dependence
Alcohol Health and Research World
  (journal) 71
Alexander, Shoshana 23–24, 111, 112
American Psychological Association
  56, 108
anger
   of abuse victims 78
   blended family and 52

codependency and 72
constructive expression of 20
coping with mismanaged 67–69
divorce and 46
dysfunctional family and 62, 63,
   64–69, 77, 60
as grief stage 41–42
"anger log" 68
anxiety 78
artificial insemination 7
assertive behavior 68, 87
attachment disorder 80
avoidance 65

B

bargaining 42
battered women *see* domestic abuse
belittling remarks 76
Berry, Dawn Bradley 84–86
Big Brothers/Big Sisters 106–7
biological parent *see* birth parent
biracial children 8–9, 33
birth control 103, 110
birth parent 33–34, 35, 96–97
   pros and cons of search for 96–98
bisexual partners *see* homosexuality
blame, abuse and 82, 85
blended families 4, 5–6
   adjustment tips 51–52
   stepsiblings 6, 12, 29–30, 50
blowing up 66
Blum, Debra 104
Brewster, Susan 77–78, 84–85
brothers *see* siblings
Brown University 74–75

C

caregivers *see* adult caregivers
change management 17
child development 80, 110
Christian-Jewish intermarriages 58
classmate bonds 111

131